TARLA'S LOG

2 0 1 0

BEING THE ACCOUNT OF A SINGLE-HANDED
VOYAGE IN A HEAVENLY TWINS CATAMARAN

FRANCIS DOUGLAS

First published in 2011 by
Claddagh Boats Ltd.

Copyright © 2011 Claddagh Boats Ltd.

A CIP Catalogue of this book is available from
the British Library

ISBN: 978-0-9568047-0-9

CHANDLER
BOOK DESIGN

Cover designed and typeset in Bembo 11pt
www.chandlerbookdesign.co.uk

Printed in Great Britain by
Ashford Colour Press Ltd.

DEDICATION

This book is dedicated to my partner
Anne Harrington who has made me
so happy over the past three years.

To Rachel & Roger
with love from
Francis xxx
4th March, 2011
The International
Day of the Book!!!!

CONTENTS

INTRODUCTION

This is the slightly edited and "embellished" log of a single-handed voyage in my catamaran "Tarla" from Walton-on-the-Naze, Essex, England to Le Port de Foleux, Beganne, Brittany, France in June/July 2010. I kept a very detailed account because I felt that it would provide "raw data" for future discussion and a partial analysis of this data can be found in the twelve Appendices which make up almost one fifth of this book.

With every voyage, however long or short, much thought must go into the planning in terms of making certain that, as far as possible, all eventualities have been catered for. This process has in fact been continuous since I purchased the "Tarla" in 2005.

This voyage could not have taken place without the help of others to all of whom I would like to express my profound thanks. In particular I would like to thank Richard and Steve Wyatt and Steve Grey of Bedwell's Boatyard, Walton-on-the-Naze, Essex for working on, and looking after, the "Tarla" during the past four years. Steve Grey used his exceptional skills to install the engine, fit the central heating and reinforce the mast-step as well as carrying out many other important tasks for me. Thanks are also due to Martin Evans for his friendship, his surveying of the "Tarla" and his overseeing of much of her restoration. Finally, I am extremely grateful to Anne and my two children,

Niall and Aoife for their ongoing support and for their work as the "back-up team".

The "Tarla", for those that are interested, is a Heavenly Twins Catamaran 8 metres by 4.2 metres, drawing less than 1 metre and weighing about 3 tons. In theory she can sleep 6 people but is much better with 2! She is rigged as a cutter (3 sails) and has a Solé diesel engine driving two hydraulic motors for the twin propellers. Consumption of Diesel is between 1 litre and 1 ½ litres per hour at 5 knots and she carries 100 litres when the tanks are full. Hence she has a range of approx 350 miles under power alone. Her maximum speed under power, or sail, is about 7 knots.

I arrived in Walton on Saturday 22nd of May (my daughter Aoife's birthday) and the "Tarla" was finally launched on Wednesday the 2nd of June. Wednesday the 2nd of June was spent fitting-out and stepping the mast. Thursday the 3rd of June was employed adjusting all the rigging and bending on the sails and in the evening I went for a trial sail with my sister Rachel and her husband Roger. While out in Hamford Water we met the Thames sailing barge "Reminder" (Master Richard Titchener) and the two ships companies waved to each other with enthusiasm!

My intention, when I set sail, was to leave the "Tarla" in the Port of Étel in Southern Brittany and then to return in the Summer of 2011 to explore that coast in depth. As I describe later Étel was not to be my destination and I ended up in the beautiful Port of Foleux instead.

Friday the 4th of June was spent putting right as many of the things possible which had been discovered from the trial sail. One of the sad things that I had to do was to saw up the "trim tab" which I had spent almost a week making at Easter because it wouldn't work with the push-pull autopilot which I had (autopilot not sensitive enough). Fortunately, I already have an autopilot that drives the wheel but it uses a lot of electricity and doesn't like it when things get rough. If you are on your own the freedom given by the autopilot steering is immense. It allows you to get on with the navigation, keep a lookout, make cups of tea etc.

As the sun sank and I eat my last meal in Walton with Rachel and Roger I felt that I had done all that I could in way of preparation. The voyage would be the test of my deficiencies and oversights.

WALTON-ON-THE-NAZE TO RAMSGATE (Pegwell Bay)

*"All men are mad who go to sea
when they could stay ashore".*

**Dr. Johnson in Boswell's
"Life of Dr. Samuel Johnson".**

got up on Saturday the 5th of June at 0300 hours and made out my passage plan to Pegwell Bay in Kent (near Ramsgate) and checked the weather forecast. My hope was that the forecast would be correct and that there would be 2 days of Easterly winds. I would then anchor overnight in Pegwell bay when the tide was foul and continue on with a fair current towards Eastbourne on Sunday.

The tides around Ramsgate, Deal and Dover run at up to 2 knots or more. If you are making 5 knots through the water with a favourable 2 knot tide your speed over the ground is 7 knots while if you are stemming a 2 knot foul tide at the same speed through the water your speed over the ground drops to 3 knots. This makes a big difference! Tides are important and so is navigation as this area is full of sandbanks with many wrecks from the days of old.

So I sailed from Walton at 0600 hours on Saturday the 5th of June and by 0658 I was rounding Pye End buoy. Cork Sand buoy was reached at 0747 and I altered course to 130 deg. True For Kentish Knock East Cardinal buoy which I reached at 1212.

On the way I passed several large ships crossing my course bound for the London River. I then set my course for the Elbow buoy off the North Foreland in Kent which I passed at 1443. I had thus crossed the Thames Estuary in a Sunny haze with visibility at about 2 miles. It was motor-sailing all the way hard on the wind (which was about Force 2). The sea was smooth, and apart from the noise of the engine, it was a pleasant trip. I saw through the mist row upon row of windmills which are part of the Warwick Energy Group on the Drill Stone off the Kent coast. None of them were turning!

From the Elbow buoy I headed for the Gull buoy off Ramsgate which I reached at 1518. I then followed the buoys towards the entrance of Ramsgate harbour veering off, just before the entrance, into Pegwell Bay. A mile and a half further on from the entrance to Ramsgate harbour I caught a fisherman's lobster pot rope round my starboard propeller and found myself anchored by the stern! Nothing daunted!!! I stripped to my shirt and under-pants, rigged a rope ladder over the side, and brandishing a very sharp knife climbed into the sea. I cut the "Tarla" free and as soon as she was released the tide and wind started to move her towards a sandbank. I climbed the rope ladder (with difficulty) put the port motor into gear and steered her towards what I thought was a good position to anchor behind a sandbank (although all around it looked like the open sea and I was a mile and a half from land). Having anchored I again climbed down the rope ladder and had the much more difficult job of hanging onto the ladder so as not to be swept away while at the same time trying to reach two feet under the water to cut the rope away from the propeller shaft where it was jammed. (The current was sweeping past at 1 to 2 knots while all this was happening). Eventually, when I thought that my arm would fall off, from the effort of "hanging on", I succeeded and with the last of my strength climbed back on board. As I wrote in the log "THANK GOD I still have the strength to lift my body weight with my arms alone". Cold and wet I stripped off and dried myself before putting on plenty of warm clothes. My pleasure at my success far exceeded my feelings of fear.

Having cooked a meal of tinned peas, tinned carrots and red salmon all mixed up together followed by a piece of Anne's cake (which has half a bottle of whiskey in it!) and all washed down with a glass of red wine I wrote the following:

"Anchored out here in Pegwell Bay is in some sense the fulfilment of a boyhood dream. Who could ever have a happier moment? To sit out here in the cockpit as the sun goes down and stare at the mast and the rigging as the stars come out. The great sailing ships of the 18th and 19th centuries used to anchor in the Downs opposite Deal which is not far from here. They anchored while waiting for a fair wind for London or to take on stores or passengers. The ships of the Honourable East India Company would drop down from the Thames to undertake the latter before sailing to India. Opposite where I sit with the twinkling lights ashore is the ancient port of Sandwich, one of the Cinque Ports, whose noted Earl, who could not tear himself away from the gambling table, invented the fast food business. As the tide drops and the evening wears on the "Tarla" gains the shelter of the drying sandbank in front of us and as often happens the wind drops at dusk. The sea is calm, I light the anchor light and turn in. I have been awake for 21 hours."

At 0200 hours on Sunday the 6th of June (4 hours later) I was woken by a helicopter with a searchlight shining down on me! He flew over and didn't stop so I imagine that I was not the cause of his trip although now-days it is rare to see a yacht anchored off the coast. At 0300 hours the wind suddenly increased from a flat calm. There was lashing rain, followed by thunder and lightening and more rain and visibility at times was down to 100 yards. I stayed awake on anchor watch! As the wind continued the sea started to get up but then as suddenly as it had started the wind stopped leaving just rain and visibility down to about a mile. I started my computer and with the dongle achieved internet connection and thus discovered that there was a small craft warning out concerning strong winds in the area from the North Foreland to Eastbourne which had certainly not been there the night before! This was confirmed by the BBC shipping forecast at 0520.

I decided to go into Ramsgate. So, in the pouring rain, I entered the Royal Harbour and tied up alongside a French yacht who shortly afterwards told me he was leaving! I found another berth and reported to the Marina office at 0800. On the basis of the recent weather forecasts for strong West or Southwest winds (on the nose for Eastbourne) I paid him 38 pounds 40 for a two day stay. I rang Anne, Aoife and Niall and had fish and chips for supper followed by a pint of bitter in the Royal Temple Yacht Club.

Today, Monday the 7th of June I went shopping and cleaned the outside of the "Tarla" which was filthy from being in the boatyard all winter.

I propose to leave Ramsgate tomorrow morning at 0400 to catch the tide to Eastbourne.

2
RAMSGATE
TO EASTBOURNE

R amsgate is an historic harbour and can trace its history back to the "Great Storm" of 1753 when Parliament passed an act for the construction of a new harbour. King George IV granted it the name of "Royal" Harbour when he was so impressed with the town's hospitality when he embarked, with the Royal Squadron, from Ramsgate to Hanover. Prior to this Ramsgate was one of the main embarkation ports during the Napoleonic wars resulting in many of the town's streets being named after the campaigns of this period including the main thoroughfare "Military Road". The promenades and crescents of the town that overlook the harbour were all built during this period.

The "Sailors' Church" and Harbour Mission was built by Canon Eustace Brennan, Vicar of Christ Church, Ramsgate in 1878. He saw the need for spiritual guidance and physical help for the men and boys who made up the crews of the sailing smacks fishing out of Ramsgate at that time. Their work at the time was, of course, extremely dangerous and many died or were injured. The young apprentices on these fishing craft were known as "Smack Boys". When they went ashore they were provided for by Canon Brennan in rooms above the "Sailors' Church" and later in the "Smack Boys' Home" next door. The latter is easily identified by the fact that it still has written on it in big letters "The Ramsgate Home for Smack Boys" although now it is occupied by a yacht broker!

Nevertheless, this home was later occupied by sailors who had been rescued from the Goodwin Sands and during the First World War some 3,300 survivors were treated there. To-day visitors to the "Sailors' Church can enjoy seeing the collection of ships models and paintings and during the summer months refreshments are provided by church members.

Ramsgate is, of course, also famous for the part it played in "Operation Dynamo" where the "Small Ships" set out to recue over 300,000 troops from the beaches of Dunkirk in 1940. [The 70 year "re-enactment" recently took place from Ramsgate]. About 40,000 of these troops landed at Ramsgate. Of the 765 vessels that went to the aid of the British and French troops almost a third were lost. Today the "Sundowner", one of the "Little Ships" and star of the film "Dunkirk", is kept in Ramsgate as a reminder.

I left Ramsgate at 0350 hrs on Tuesday the 8th of June, having got up at 0230 to prepare for the trip. I left "Sundowner" perched on top of the harbour wall and headed out into the English Channel at first light.

I had to compromise. On the one hand I wanted all the tide that I could get to help me on my way. On the other hand I did not wish to navigate in such tricky waters in the dark. Thus I forwent about three hours of fair tide. Secondly, the weather forecast was better for Wednesday but that would mean that I would lose another hour of fair tide if I wished to sail in daylight and I would then have difficulty getting past Dover. As it turned out I just managed to pass Dover before the tide turned against me.

Passing through the "Downs" close to the town of Deal I was reminded of the early pioneers of single handed sailing. E.E. Midleton who wrote "The Cruise of the Kate" in 1869 became the first man to sail single handed round Britain by way of the Crinan Canal. The Kate weighed 5 tons and was 25.5 feet overall with a 7 feet beam (2 tons heavier than the "Tarla" with about the same length but only half the beam). He spent many hours rowing as well as sailing and subsisted off biscuits and a little sherry. He tried to come into harbour each night (when he usually took a pilot) and put up at a hotel where he became very cross if they did not accept one of his cheques as he felt it impugned his honour as a gentleman. Midleton speaks in his book on the voyage as having passed a large fleet of merchantmen anchored in the Downs which were spread over two or three miles off Deal. I saw three vessels, and none at anchor, before I reached Dover!

Midleton's inspiration for his lone voyage was John McGregor who published "The Voyage Alone in the Yawl 'Rob Roy' in 1867. He was a publicist and benefactor (which Midleton was not) who sailed his 21 foot boat from Limehouse, London to Dover, thence to Boulogne and along the North coast of France to the Seine, up the Seine to Paris, down again to Havre and from Havre across the channel to Littlehampton, the Solent and thence back to London along the English coast. It took him three and a half months.

McGregor's father was appointed Inspector General of the Irish Constabulary in 1838 and went to live in Drumcondra, Dublin where the young McGregor was bought up. After attending Trinity College, Dublin. John moved to Trinity College, Cambridge where he rowed in his college eight. He wrote for "Punch", went to London and read for the Bar and in 1850 took his degree of M.A. from Cambridge. He was a member of the "ragged boys" committee which endeavoured to help street urchins and in 1848 he met Carlyle (author of Cromwell's life etc.) in Drumcondra. He always maintained that Carlyle was the seminal influence on his life.

Due to his interest in "ragged boys" he founded the Shoeblack Society which provided employment for street urchins. Shoeblacks wore scarlet coats and were a familiar sight in London to people, like my Grandmother, in the early years of the 20th Century. McGregor also came up with a scheme whereby poor girls would scrub peoples' steps for payment but it never took off.

In May 1865 he thought up the idea of making a lengthy voyage in a canoe. He designed the canoe himself. His book "A Thousand Miles in the Rob Roy Canoe on Twenty Lakes and Rivers of Europe" (1866) made a huge impact on the young men of Victorian England. He then decided to form a canoe club to encourage this type of activity and hit on the very bright idea of inviting the Prince of Wales to become its first President. Thus the Royal Canoe club was formed and members flocked in and formed branches all over the Country. McGregor even designed a special outfit for men and women to go canoeing in! The Voyage Alone in the Yawl Rob Roy was an extension of his ideas on canoes.

As I sailed from Ramsgate at 0350 the wind was SW Force 1 and it was raining with moderate visibility. Although not yet sunrise the Eastern sky was becoming lighter. By 0441, with a fair tide under me and the engine running at 1400 revs and no sail set, the West Goodwin Buoy was abeam to Starboard and I was in the Downs. I was making 5.9 knots through the water and 7.2 knots over the ground. By 0452 the town of Deal was abeam visible, because of its street lights, through the mist. At 0520 visibility closed in because of the rain. The South Foreland was visible indistinctly to Starboard at 0523 when I also passed the South Goodwin Buoy and thus left the Downs. The wind was now SSE Force 2. I set the two headsails and continued on with the engine running at 1400 revs and altered course to 230 Degrees (True). At 0621 I was abeam of Dover Harbour with a stream of ships passing me at right angles on their way in and out. (Dover is one of the busiest harbours in the World and it is always a concern crossing the paths of big fast ships in a very small slow one). Having passed Dover about one and a half miles offshore I was exactly over the channel tunnel at 0700 with the wind unchanged, revs increased to 1500, speed through the water 6 knots and speed over the ground 5.4 knots. The tide had turned!

However, the sun had come out and the rain had stopped and I had to take off my shell-top as I was too warm! The scenery with the white cliffs of Dover with the sun shining on them was absolutely stunning. It really was most enjoyable sitting there in the cockpit drinking a cup of tea and eating a piece of Anne's cake and watching it all go by. I was now steering 240 Degrees and heading into Dymchurch bay to avoid some of the foul tide which turned out to be a mistake as I shall relate in a moment. By 0736 Folkstone Harbour light was abeam to starboard and speed through the water was 5.8 knots with speed over the ground being 4.8 knots. The engine had been slowed to 1400 revs and the two headsails were just pulling in the Southerly Force 2 wind. By 0800 it was spitting rain again and the sky had turned black. The rain then came in heavy, the wind veered to the SSW and increased to Force 5 and because of my earlier decision I could no longer lay my course to weather Dungeness and was driven further into Dymchurch bay. The land was blotted out by the rain and all one could see was about half a mile of increasingly rough sea all around. However, I knew that as I got closer to the headland that is Dungeness I would come under its shelter so I made up my mind to anchor close to the shore and wait until the tide turned in my favour before trying to round the headland. Thus I studied the chart and concluded that on my present course I would be anchoring in St. Mary's bay and there seemed to be good holding ground and no obvious hazards. But, before doing this, because I was loath to stop, I furled the two headsails at 0900 and headed directly into the wind on a course of 200 Degrees True in order to clear Dungeness. With the engine at 1500 revs the speed through the water was 4 knots. Speed over the ground was three knots and we were burning fuel and not getting anywhere quickly! Dungeness was seven miles away. The wind suddenly dropped to Force 1, the sun came out and I observed that since losing sight of the ships off Dover I had only seen three other vessels---2 fishing boats and one sailing yacht. Not a lot of people out!

By 1020 Dungeness nuclear power station was clearly in sight on the headland and I had also sighted two more sailing yachts coming round it. I was now doing, because of the reduction in wind strength, some 4.5 knots through the water with 3.3 knots over the ground. The wind was now South Force 1 to 2 but Tarla certainly knows how to hobbyhorse (Rock backwards and forwards) as, at times, she put her bows completely under the seas knocked up by the recent squall. Salt spray covered the forward windows and stuck fast making it difficult to look out of them inside the cabin.

By 1100 hours Dungeness lighthouse with its black and white stripes and its light still winking was abeam to Starboard. By 1141 I had reached buoy CS3 which marks the edge of the big ship channel and I altered course to 250 degrees (True). As I did so a huge container ship overtook me on the other side of the buoy. I set the staysail but I was pointing too close to the wind to set the jib and continued on under engine. At 1200 I eased her off the wind enough to set the jib and reduced revs to 1400. Now doing 5.8 knots through the water and 5.2 knots over the ground. The tide is starting to turn in my favour once again!

At 1230 I marked my position on the chart as I have done hourly or half hourly since I sailed from Ramsgate. At 1315 I eased off the engine revs to 1200 to conserve fuel. Now making 4.6 knots through the water and 5.1 knots over the ground. By 1345 it had become very bouncy pushing into a head sea but the sun had come out again and the coast looked very beautiful. At 1400 I eased off to 1000 revs which is only just above "tick-over" and was motor-sailing at 4.5 knots on course for the outfall buoy off St. Leonards. At 1500 Hastings Tower was abeam and I was trying to remember all that I knew about 1066 and all that! At 1545 St. Leonards outfall buoy was abeam and I altered course to

255 degrees (True) for Sovereign Harbour, Eastbourne. Increased revs to 1300. Furled jib as wind was almost on the nose again and was making 4.3 knots through the water with the "Tarla" hobby-horsing badly. She was making good 4 knots over the ground. At 1615 the tide had truly turned against me once again (4.5 Knots through the water and 4 knots over the ground) and at 1745 I was finally approaching Sovereign Harbour 66 miles from Ramsgate. I rigged mooring lines and put out fenders and motored into the lock at 1805. At 1830 I locked out into the harbour and was moored up by 1900. I then received a very welcome phone call from Anne although she couldn't have known that I had just arrived. I cooked beans and smoked herring all mixed up and followed it with a bowl of berries all washed down with a bottle of red wine. I went to bed at 2200 hours and slept like a log.

Wednesday the 9th June, 2010 turned out to be a wonderful sunny day with no wind. I awoke at 0730 and had breakfast. I then sorted out a number of problems that had arisen the day before one of which was that my main halyard had managed to fasten itself around the steaming light 20 feet above the deck. By placing the ladder against the mast and climbing to the top of it my head was approximately 12 feet above the deck Then using the boathook with the mooring grabber tied to it I managed by poking and pushing to free the halyard. I Rang Solar Traders to order another solar panel as with two 32 watt panels I think they will provide enough electricity to run the fridge (This has since proved to be the case with electricity to spare). I then had a very pleasant cup of coffee in the cockpit with the sunshades rigged and while I was there a Westerly Centaur being motored round the harbour by a man with a lady on the foredeck came close by and the lady said "Hello Ireland"! She seemed absolutely delighted to see the Irish flag flying in Eastbourne and a boat registered in Cork (Easily seen because "Tarla Cork" is written with big letters on the stern!)

From 1200 to 1500 I walked into Eastbourne (about 2 miles from Sovereign Harbour) and back again. While there I purchased 5 shirts, 10 pairs of underpants, 1 belt, 1 pair of trousers and 1 pair of shorts. Eastbourne is one of those places which one imagines is full of retired Colonels sitting in deck chairs by the bandstand while the orchestra plays "Soldiers of the Queen". As it turned out the Colonels must all be going round in disguise and there was no orchestra at the bandstand! Sovereign harbour, on the other hand, is two thirds full of large ugly plastic motor yachts owned by middle aged men who arrive in open topped sports cars with 20 year old girlfriends on their arm. The harbour was created with a digger and the very expensive tall rise flats overlook the water and the yachts. I keep telling myself that I shouldn't like it but I do. Perhaps it has something to do with the fact that the yachts that arrive and depart each day have some very interesting people on them and I have always found the marina staff very friendly here and they have excellent showers and facilities.

From 1500 to 1600 I went to the yacht chandlers and purchased a 2 pin plug and went shopping for food and drink at the ASDA supermarket. From 1600 to 1700 I had lunch sitting in the sun in the cockpit (A sandwich purchased in ASDA and a pint of beer from my fridge). At 1800 went for a shower and ended the day by going for a meal in the Harvester restaurant. At 2200 I turned in.

On Thursday the 10th of June I got up and had a cup of tea at 0600 hours. From 0600 to 0800 I packed my clothes for my trip to London. This was the day that I was to join the Thames Sailing Barge the "Reminder" in Limehouse Basin, London (The place where 'Rob Roy' McGregor set off in his yawl almost 150 years ago). I looked up the times of trains and the weather on the internet.

At 0900 had a fascinating talk with a fisherman from Pevensey Bay who had spent all his life fishing off the open beach. He had a liver transplant four years ago and is now 72 and is working as a rubbish collector in Sovereign Harbour. His fishing boat was elm planked and weighed three tons. Two of them dragged her up the beach using an electric capstan(One H.P. with suitable reduction gearing) and pulled her off to a buoy just off the beach with the boats own capstan (normally used to work the fishing gear) when they were launching her. A big concrete wheel was buried at low tide, using the digger that came to repair the groins to stop coastal erosion, and this anchored the buoy offshore at high tide to take the necessary strains. He had an air cooled diesel on his boat and when they beached through the waves he kept it pushing ahead so that his crew could run up and get the capstan wire. The engine being engaged in pushing the boat ahead stopped the boat being dragged back out to sea by the undertow.

I caught the 1247 from Eastbourne to Victoria and went to my eldest sister's Ruth's house near Bow End. There I met my brother-in-law Bill and after a cup of tea we both walked to the local Dockland light Railway station where we took a train to Limehouse. The barge, the "Reminder" was by far the largest craft in the basin being over 80 feet long with her mainmast towering into the sky. The barge had been chartered by the Engineering Council (where my sister Ruth works) from "Sea-change" which is a registered charity of which I am a trustee. "Sea-change" had chartered the "Reminder" from "Topsail Charters" of Maldon, Essex. For those that are interested much more information can be obtained from the web (including pictures). "Sea-change" has as its purpose the provision of developmental opportunities for a range of people including the disadvantaged. To this end it proposes to build a new Thames Sailing Barge (without an engine) which will be capable of carrying cargo. The last sailing barge to earn her living purely under sail was the "Cambria" which ceased trading in 1970. The new barge will be the first full-size barge to be built since the early 1930's.

That evening we went to a pub by the River Thames for a meal and sat beside the window where at high tide it had to be shut to stop the spray and waves from the passing boats coming in! We all went to bed on the barge after midnight having consumed a lot of alcohol.

The next day, Friday the 11th of June, we sailed at mid-day locking out of Limehouse basin into the River Thames. The crew consisted of ten of us as passengers, Richard Titchener as Master, Francis (not me!) as Mate, and Don and "Stretch" (who we picked up at Gravesend) as professional crew. We moored up to the "Camel" in Gravesend at about 1500 hours after a very pleasant trip downriver where we passed Greenwich, the millennium dome, the Thames tidal barrier and so on. The "Marjorie" moored up on the other side of the "Camel" shortly afterwards. I should explain that the "Camel" is a large "dumb" lighter owned by the Port of London authority and permanently moored off the park in Gravesend. There was no sign of "The Lady of the Lea" which was the third competitor.

On Saturday the 12th of June we were all up at 0500 hours preparing for the passage match which was a race from Gravesend to Harwich (56 miles). The "Lady of the Lea" had appeared from nowhere and was moving down river towards the starting line which we all crossed shortly after 0630 hours. Ten hours later at 1630 hours we had just tacked off Clacton Pier, the Marjorie was eight miles ahead and the "Lady of the Lea" was so far behind that we had lost sight of her (but she is much smaller). At 1910 we crossed the finish line with the "Marjorie" beating us by about an hour. [She was almost becalmed so we were catching up with her fast at the end!] The "Lady of the Lea" retired and started her engine reaching Harwich about 2200 hours. [Harwich marked the finish line for the Barge Match]. On the way in, approaching Harwich, one could clearly see Martin Evans' beautiful double bow fronted "Captain's House" standing proudly by the church. (Martin was the man that surveyed the

"Tarla" when I bought her and has played a significant part in her restoration since then). That night we anchored off Pin Mill in beautiful surroundings and the "Lady of the Lea" joined us before mid-night. The "Marjorie" had already gone on up to the wet dock in Ipswich.

The next morning, Sunday the 13th of June we sailed down the river Orwell surrounded by yachts, also sailing, in warm sunshine. We passed the beautiful little church at Levington, near where Authur Ransome (the author of "Swallows and Amazons") used to live, and then retraced our steps going up with the flood tide to Ipswich under sail and only starting the engine at the last minute before going into the wet dock and mooring up in front of the "Marjorie".

We left in a taxi at about 1500 and took the fast train to London. I stayed with Ruthie and Bill for the night and caught the 1047 from Victoria to Eastbourne. I then cleaned ship ready for the visit of Michael and Judith Harrington who sold the "Tarla" to me 5 years ago this coming September. They both arrived at 1700 and with their usual generosity came bearing a fruit cake which Judith had cooked and soaked in Brandy and a signed copy of Michael's book which he has just published entitled "Pacific Odyssey: Lane's Story by Michael Harrington". They also brought me a bottle of red wine. After drinks on the "Tarla" we adjourned to the Thai restaurant where we had the most excellent meal. One never minds paying money, if one has it, for really good food and service. I returned to the "Tarla", after they had left, and had a really long phone conversation with Anne before turning in.

Tuesday the 15th of June was very windy but sunny. I got up at 0730 and went shopping. Upon my return I prepared for Michael and Judith who were coming for coffee. They duly arrived at 1100 hours towing a small trolley in which they had further gifts. They very generously gave me their sailing waterproofs, sea-boots and gloves together with a hardback copy of Marin

Marie's "Wind Aloft" which describes his single handed voyage across the Atlantic in the cutter the "Winnibelle" in the 1930's. (Marin Marie, a Frenchman, was also the first person to cross the Atlantic single handed in a motor boat which was called the "Arielle"). We spent a very pleasant time chatting until they both left me at 1230. I spent the rest of the afternoon working on this communication, cooked myself a meal and went to bed at 2200hrs.

The strong Northerly winds, which blew all day, are forecast to continue tomorrow so it looks like Thursday the 17th of June will be the earliest day for departure from Eastbourne!

3
EASTBOURNE
TO BEMBRIDGE I.O.W.

I n the morning I walked into Eastbourne and bought a small camera from Argos at a special offer price of £69. [By the time I had bought a case to keep it in, extra memory cards and batteries this had come to £108 !]. I was back from my walk to Eastbourne by 1200 and had lunch on the "Tarla". From 1230 to 1500 I had a snooze and then at 1530 went to the ASDA super-market to buy stores. From 1630 onwards I carried out a number of small jobs. I listened to the shipping forecast and having heard that there were inshore gale warnings for the next 24 hours I decided not to sail tomorrow. So I made a salad, drank wine and went to bed at 2200 suffering from sinus problems due to an allergic reaction to the dust being blown up by the strong Northerly winds!

On Thursday 17th June I got up having slept well, despite the sinus, and felt much better. Had breakfast and sorted out the recharging of my various bits of electrical equipment--- handheld VHF Radio, Spotlight, Mobile Phone, etc. I spent the morning pottering around. Had coffee and went again to ASDA where I bought plastic storage boxes and glue and spent the afternoon fixing things on my list of "Things to Do". At 1700 I went for a shower after which I moved the "Tarla" alongside the refuelling berth where I purchased 56 litres of Diesel (£50-07); 5 litres of petrol for the dinghy outboard engine (£6-46); One refilled cylinder of "Camping Gaz" (£21-95) and paid for the cost of berthing for 10 days (£230). Total bill £308-48. I then made out the passage plan from Sovereign Harbour Eastbourne to Bembridge Harbour, Isle of Wight. The starting point for the passage plan is "What time is it high tide at Dover?" The next question is "Is it spring tides or neap tides?" From this information one can then consult the tidal atlas and determine when and where one will have favourable currents. The next problem is that Bembridge Harbour is a drying harbour with a buoyed (although unlit) channel. [One knows this by looking Bembridge up in the Pilot Book even though one has never been there]. One thus needs to enter Bembridge at or near high water during daylight. High water at Bembridge is 14 minutes later than High Water at Dover. Your next problem is how long is it going to take to cover the total distance of 60 miles? At 5 knots it will take 12 hours but especially if you are sailing it may take longer. It will certainly take longer if a foul tide is pushing you back! High tide at Dover on Friday the 18th of June was at 1526 plus 14 minutes for Bembridge plus one hour for British Summer Time equals 1640. So I had to arrive at Bembridge no later than two hours after high water and preferably before that. However, my tidal atlas showed me that as I approached the Owers Buoy there would be a strong current against me which would set me back. At the same time I could not avoid this if I wished to arrive at Bembridge at high tide. I decided in the light of all of the above to lock out of Sovereign Harbour at 0300 and be off Beachy Head by HW Dover at 0400. This would give me a favourable tide for the first six hours with a foul (and stronger) tide for the six hours after. Finally, I noted the courses to be steered as follows:

"Course from Sovereign Harbour outer buoy to turning point (chosen by me) off Beachy Head 200 Deg. True. Dist 6 miles. Course from turning point to Owers Buoy 265 Deg. True. Dist 37 miles. Course from Owers Buoy to Bembridge Ledge Buoy 280 Deg. True. Dist 14 miles. Course from Bembridge

Ledge Buoy to St. Helen's Fort 310 Deg. True. Dist 2 miles."

This completed the "passage plan" and is a process which I go through in meticulous detail before each stage of the trip. The other equally important job to carry out before starting is to obtain as much information as you can about the weather and "if in doubt" don't go! It doesn't have to be a gale or fog. A headwind of Force 3 can stop me too! To this end I listen to the shipping forecast, consult Navtex, fire up my laptop computer with its dongle and use my common sense by consulting the sky which often proves to be the most reliable!

Before refuelling I met a chap called John Holroyde, his sister Anne and her husband who invited me aboard their ferro-cement sailing yacht the "Touchstone". I thought that it must be Mike Peyton's (the famous nautical cartoonists) former vessel. However, it turned out that it was a smaller version 34ft 11ins long with 10ft 6ins beam and 4ft 6ins draught designed by the same designer Alan Hill. I was most impressed with her. Ferro-cement done well is obviously a very sound form of construction and is much under-rated. I took photos of her inside and out with my new camera. At 1900 I had a glass of wine and a meal of bread and cheese and finished the day with a loverly long phone call from Anne.

Friday 18th June, 2010.
At 0200 I got up. Found my Musto shell suit and put it on as it was cold outside. The bottom of the "shell suit" is like a "babygrow" with the arms cut off. The jacket goes on top of this so that one's middle gets two layers giving extra warmth. The beauty of it is that it is wind resistant and showerproof. I made a cup of tea and eat a bowl of shreddies. I drank more tea and at 0230 was still drinking tea! At 0235 I switched on all the instruments except the radar (Port control doesn't like it!) and singled up mooring lines. At 0245 I started the engine and switched on my navigation lights as it was still pitch black.

At 0250 I was in the lock and at 0325. I passed the outer buoy and took my departure, I hoisted the mainsail, streamed the log (set at zero) and set the course for my turning point off Beachy Head of 200 Deg. True. The lights of Eastbourne were twinkling away to starboard and the dark shape of Beachy Head loomed out of the murk ahead. The sails were now slatting due to lack of wind. Wind North Force ½. By 0400 there is red in the Eastern sky and a beautiful dawn commences. I am reminded of a sentence in the information booklet for my pre-sea training course for the Merchant Navy at the School of Navigation, The University of Southampton, which said that cadets on the sail training vessel---The 80ft ketch the "Halcyon" (now-days featured on the web)---would see their first dawn of the many that they would see in their long professional lives at sea. Beachy Head is a big white headland that dominates. According to the "Pilot" there is a race off the end of it so my turning point is designed to take account of this. At 0405 I can see the stripes on the lighthouse which look in this first light as if they are black and white. At 0430 with the log reading 6.30 miles from Sovereign outer buoy I altered course to 265 Deg. True. For the Owers Buoy 37 miles distant. I stopped the engine as the wind had now increased a bit to a Force 2/3 on the beam. We were sailing at last! At 0445 I realised that Beachy Head lighthouse had red and white stripes not black and white as I had thought earlier! I confirmed this by looking it up in the almanac. At 0500 I made another cup of tea and eat a large chunk of Anne's cake. At 0530 the log read 10.68 with speed through the water being 5 knots and the speed over the ground 5.6 knots. The tide had turned! I plotted Tarla's position on the chart and returned to the cockpit to see light hazy clouds in streaks covering the blue sky. It all looked pretty settled. Out at sea, almost hull down on the horizon, one huge container ship after another was steaming down channel in the shipping lane. At 0600 I could see the Newhaven Ferry inward bound. I altered course to 280 Deg.

True. Remembering the importance of the "weather gauge" (always stay up-wind of your course if you can). By 0630 the Ferry was almost into Newhaven and I had made good 6.2 nautical miles over the ground in the last hour under sail. I gave a metaphorical wave to Mike and Judith Harrington (the previous owners of Tarla) who live in Peacehaven quite close to the sea. I calculated that as I was seven miles from the coast they were about seven and a half miles away. The wind was strengthening. Now a good Force 4 from the North West and thus forward of the beam. Tarla was going like a train with salt spray coming over the bows! Speed through the water climbed to 6.5 knots and speed over the ground to 7.5 knots. She made the occasional "thump" as a sea hit the bottom of the bridgedeck but there was nothing alarming. Brighton is now lit up by the morning sun.

Brighton reminded me that it had been made fashionable by the Prince Regent who had been instrumental in the construction of the very ornate pier. Brighton was also home to the University of Sussex, the first of the "new" Universities which took in its first undergraduates in 1960. I myself attended the last "new" University—The New University of Ulster---which came after York and Sterling when it opened its doors in 1968. The other thing which Brighton has from the seafaring perspective is its very safe and entirely artificial harbour which was opened by Her Majesty the Queen in 1979.

By 0650 the wind had eased off and speed through the water had decreased to 4.5 knots with a bumpy ride. I made another cup of tea and this time drank it without eating cake! By 0730 I was abeam of Brighton which was 8.7 miles away. By 0745 the wind had dropped to Force 2 and come round to the North (on the beam). Speed through the water 4.5 knots. Shortly after the wind increased again although it was now forward of the beam. Speed through the water rose to 6.2 knots with a speed over the ground of 6.7 knots. [17 miles to go to the Owers Buoy]. Shoreham is now abeam to starboard some 9.3 miles distant.

Shoreham is very much a commercial port concerned with timber, seaborne aggregates, stone and steel and according to the "pilot" apart from the delightful Yacht Club it seems to have few attractions for yachtsmen. The major problem is obtaining a berth and the "pilot" implies that this is very much a hit and miss affair.

I wrote in the log at this point "So far today I have seen one fishing vessel and one sailing yacht making for Brighton in the distance. Apart from these and the Newhaven ferry and the Container ships early on I have seen nothing else. Now there is a small ship making for Shoreham". [15 minutes later I decided that this was a large fishing trawler going nowhere!] I also sighted a yacht in the far distance setting a large headsail. At 0855 there were two yachts under sail ahead and I could see two very conspicuous tall-rise buildings in what I took to be Worthing on the Starboard bow. At 0900 the log was registered 28.75 miles from Eastbourne. Speed through the water was 5 knots and speed over the ground 5.2 knots. At 0930 the wind dropped again and speed through the water fell to 4.2 knots. At 0945 a fishing boat (Power Catamaran) passed at speed and I passed another one hauling her pots close to Port [Her number was L I 5]. Worthing is now abeam with Littlehampton broad on the Starboard bow.

Littlehampton is the home of the Hillyard boatbuilding yard which between the two World wars and after the Second World War built economical wooden sailing yachts which offered excellent value for money. This was partially the result of David Hillyard's religion which meant that he felt that it was immoral to make large profits. Many of these vessels are still afloat and greatly loved by their owners. Indeed, during the passage match on the "Reminder" we passed the "Margo" a Hillyard owned by Pat and Brian who are friends of mine from Walton-on-the-Naze.

At 1000 I altered course to 255 Deg true for the Owers Buoy as I was now upwind of my course. The wind was now dead astern and I was running goose-winged with sails out on both sides. I had to get out of my Musto shell suit bottoms because

I was too warm! At 1030 speed through the water was down to 2.3 knots and speed over the ground 2.1 knots. The tide had turned against me! By 1100 Bognor Regis was abeam and I was passed by a large fast motor yacht which set me rocking in her wake. The wind then came round on the beam. The chart-plotter showed the Owers Buoy to be 2.8 miles away. At 1200 I had lunch of goat's cheese and TUC biscuits, a banana, an apple and a cup of tea. I wrote in the log that Tarla sailed beautifully with the wind on the beam at 4 knots in very light winds. Absolutely no stress!

However, at 1230 I looked at the chart-plotter and couldn't believe my eyes! Speed over the ground was zero while speed through the water was 3.5 knots! Being the person I am I immediately thought that the chart-plotter was broken! However, having consulted the Furuno GPS which is beside the chart table which also said that speed over the ground was zero I started the engine! Speed through the water increased to 4.8 knots and 2 knots over the ground. The Ower's Buoy was finally abeam at 1315. Selsey Bill (Remember the shipping forecast "North Foreland to Selsey Bill") was abeam to starboard. I altered course for Bembridge Ledge Buoy. We were now motor-sailing hard on the wind. The Nab tower which we would leave close to Port was already in sight.

By 1445 the South Pullar Buoy was abeam to Port. The log read 51.21. I increased engine revs to 1600. Speed through the water was 6 knots and speed over the ground 5 knots. At 1547 the Nab tower was abeam to Port with the log reading 57.03. It was extremely hectic. I was crossing the shipping lane and large ships seemed to be bearing down on me from both sides!

Coming up to the Nab tower there was a Brittany Ferries ship passing less than half a mile ahead of me. A helicopter was hanging stationary above the ferry for 10 minutes at a time then flying away briefly before repeating the procedure. I presume they must have been practising taking someone off who was sick.

The wind was now directly ahead so I lowered and furled all sail. I counted 12 large merchant ships coming or going or at anchor within 2 miles of me. At 1630 Bembridge Ledge Buoy was abeam. The log read 60.78. I altered course for St. Helen's Fort. Distance 2 miles. Course 310 Deg. True. At 1655 I reached the tide gauge off the entrance and handed the log which read 62.54. I rigged mooring lines fore and aft and put out fenders on both sides and proceeded up the well marked channel into Bembridge Harbour. I moored up at 1725 beside a German motor-sailor and was the third out from the pontoon. [All the other yachts there were rafted two or three deep]. Tidied up and sent a text to Niall, Aoife, and Michael Harrington indicating my safe arrival and phoned Anne to tell her the same. I cooked baked beans with sausages and mixed them with another tin of mushy peas. Had two glasses of wine and relished the tranquillity after the voyage---particularly the stress of the last part because of having to avoid the large ships. This gave rise to thoughts concerning safety in harbour and contrasting it with "the perils of the sea", which in turn gave rise to thinking of the well known Church of England Hymn "For those in peril on the sea". All this was probably the wine talking!

The voyage resulted in 6 hours of motor-sailing and 8 hours under sail alone. Less than 10 litres of diesel were used even though at the end the engine was doing 1600 revs.

I consulted the shipping forecast using my laptop with dongle and discovered that the Inshore forecast for "Wight" was predicting Gale Force winds in the East and strong winds elsewhere. It was a flat calm in Bembridge!

At 2100 I went for a walk to the harbour office and at 2200 turned in.

Picture of the "Tarla" in Eastbourne (Sovereign Harbour)

The "Arklow Wind" which I passed at sea off the Isle of White

"Le Vieux Copain" in Cherbourg Harbour

*The Château at Tréguier under which Tom Cunliffe
rode out Hurricane Charlie in 1986*

*Peter Spry-Leverton arrives in L'Aberwrac'h
aboard the "Anadina"*

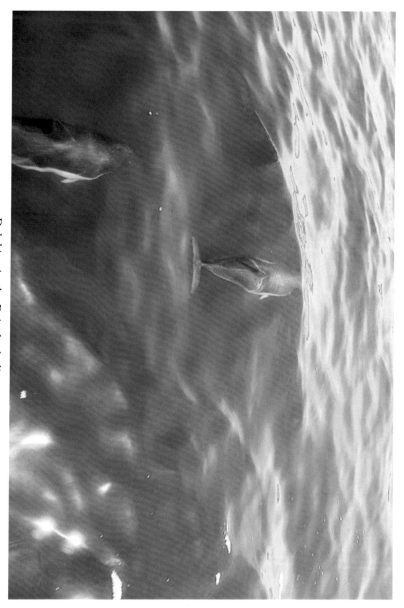

Dolphins in the Baie de Audienne

The Îles de Glénan

Port Tudy, Île de Goix

The Île de Hnout

Le Port de Foleux

4

BEMBRIDGE I.O.W.
TO CHERBOURG, FRANCE

Saturday the 19ᵗʰ of June.

At 0300 I was woken up by the sound of lashing rain and howling wind, clanking halyards and the sound of the windmill on the German motor-sailor beside me whining loudly! Given the surging of our three vessels on their warps and the fact that I was the outside vessel I could do nothing else but get up and check that everything was O.K. I had a cup of tea and read a book as the stormy sky, with that hard steely look, got brighter. The Wind was SW Force 6 and it reduced to about Force 4 after half an hour. In fact the lashing rain did me a service as it washed all the salt off my windows which had been covered by the spray when she had been "going like a train" the day before. At 0500 I went back to bed and was woken at 0700 by the boats behind me leaving. So from 0700 to 0830 I worked out my passage plan from Bembridge to Cherbourg. After this I walked to the village of St. Helens. The village however only had a very small shop despite being one and a half miles from the harbour. It had a very nice young lady in it but the supplies were limited! However, the walk was not wasted because there was an excellent second hand bookshop there where I bought three books.

St. Helens is very much a traditional English Village, centred as it is around the second largest green in the country on which is found both a cricket pitch and a football pitch.

The origins of this village derive from the Cluniac Priory, built c. 1080, the remains of which are now the site of the Priory Bay Hotel. The original village church was built circa 1200 on the seafront. It eventually became unsafe and a new church was built further inland in the 18th century. The original church tower still remains and for many years has been used as a seamark. The positions of both the priory and the church, apparently far from the village itself, are explained by the fact that the District of St. Helens was originally much larger and stretched to the edges of what is now Ryde.

St Helens has played its part in the history of the British Isles, usually due to its connection with sailing and the fact that it is a well known safe anchorage. In 1340 a French invasion force landed here but was repelled by Sir Theobald Russell. In 1346 Edward III set sail from here to invade Normandy. St Helens was famed amongst sailors for the purity of its water which, for this reason, was often collected by the navy before long voyages as it would remain fresh for longer than any other water. In addition, stones from the old church were often used to clean the decks of old sailing ships, giving rise to the practice known as "holy-stoning" the decks. In 1805 Admiral Lord Nelson's fleet gathered off the harbour entrance before setting sail for Cadiz to play its part in the Battle of Trafalgar. It is commonly accepted that Nelson's last view of England was of this village.

St Helen's Fort is situated in the Solent, just off shore. It was built between 1867 and 1880 to protect Portsmouth from French invasion. As the expected invasion didn't happen these forts, of which this is only one, became known as Palmerstone's follies! There is also a famous golf course in St. Helens which in the past was used by Royalty from all over Europe and which rivalled St Andrews in importance.

More recently many boats were built here, including motor torpedo boats, which played their part during the two great

World Wars and Bembridge Harbour was an important staging point for vessels engaged in the Normandy landings in June 1944, 66 years ago.

During my walk back from the village I visited the old church, which is a seamark, and saw where Lord Nelson had embarked for the Victory on the 14th of September 1805. Sailing past from one end of the horizon to the other were the hundreds of yachts taking part in the "Round the Island race" which proved to be an unforgettable sight.

In the afternoon I moved the "Tarla" as requested by the Marina staff and tied up beside a Prout Elite Catamaran called the "Suum Cuique". Her owners, Ted and Ginny Chalk, very kindly invited me to have dinner with them aboard their vessel at 1930. I had a very pleasant meal with them and returned aboard at 2300 and turned in.

Sunday 20th of June.

I got up at 0300 and , as usual, had a cup of tea. I shipped the compass, chart-plotter, radar etc. and singled up mooring lines. At 0420 (2 hours before HW Bembridge) I let go of the "Suum Cuique" and headed down the harbour. At 0440 I had St Helen's fort abeam and streamed the log. I altered course for Bembridge Ledge Buoy. Course 130 Deg. True. Dist 2 miles. At 0502 Bembridge Ledge buoy was abeam and I altered course to 210 Deg. True. to head for the West Princess Buoy. Dist. 1.2 miles. At 0515 the West Princess Buoy was abeam to Port and I altered course to 200 Deg. True for Cherbourg. Dist. 63 miles. Speed through the water 5.4 knots; Speed over the ground 5.1 knots. Decided to keep motoring until we cleared Culver Cliff and were comfortably into Sandown Bay where I expected the foul tide to slacken. HW Dover was at 0606 and after that I expected the tide to turn in my favour.

At 0525 Culver Cliff was abeam to Starboard. It is a very impressive big white cliff with a monument on the top of it.

Sandown bay looked very pretty in the early morning sunlight. Set the jib only with the engine at 1400 revs and Tarla was making 6 knots through the water. At 0600, having furled the jib, I bought her head to the wind and hoisted the mainsail. I sorted out the tangle of the reefing lines with the lazy-jacks--- one hand for yourself and one for the ship and all that! I certainly took great care to hang on tightly because her motion was quite "jerky" as she motored directly into the wind under autopilot. After this I put her back on course.

At 0615 I stopped the engine and set the staysail and jib. Speed through the water 5.5 knots and speed over the ground 6.2 knots. The tide has turned!

At 0630 I was broad reaching with a Northerly wind Force 2 to 3. It really was wonderful in this smooth sea with the land slipping past and the early morning sun beginning to warm me. When I hoisted the mainsail it had dumped a whole lot of water on me from the lashing rain of the previous night so I needed warming up! Another yacht is coming up astern presumably also bound for Cherbourg or Alderney. By 0642 I was abeam of Benchurch and St Catherine's lighthouse was now in sight.

At 0715 I furled the staysail and jib as the wind had dropped and set the flat-cut spinnaker. This is an equilateral triangular sail of 270 square feet designed to be used in light winds. With this set the "Tarla" was doing 4.5 knots through the water and 6.2 knots over the ground and you could hardly feel the wind. The yacht behind is now only about one quarter of a mile away. She caught up a lot while I was trying to sort out the spinnaker. She turns out to be a beautifully varnished "Colin Archer" about 36 feet long. She probably has a waterline length of about 30 feet which will give her an edge (slightly) on speed. Tarla is only 21ft 6ins on the waterline. I finally tamed the spinnaker on the "Tarla" by tacking it down to the weather bow. By 0815 the "Colin Archer" has overtaken us, although we catch up with him slightly in the gusts as we achieve 6.5 knots under mainsail and spinnaker.

We are doing 8 knots over the ground! The "Colin Archer" has now set a huge masthead balloon spinnaker but before doing so went all over the ocean zigging and zagging in front of me while they sorted it out. This involved launching the tinker tramp dinghy, retrieving the tinker tramp and a lot of moving around on deck. There appears to be two of them.

By 0830 St Catherine's Lighthouse was abeam. Speed through the water was 4.6 knots and speed over the ground 6.2. This shows how far we have been swept down channel by the tide already. I discovered at this point that the log was jammed even though the "speedo" was working (It is a Stowe log which I purchased new in the early 1980s). I reset it to zero and it seemed to work fine. How odd! In the last half hour we have covered 4.2 miles over the ground! This is fast! At 0845 I notice that a large green merchant ship has altered course for me and that he will pass under my stern which is jolly decent of him and doesn't happen very much now-days although the "Rule of the Road" still says that "Steam should give way to sail" [except where restricted by draft or width of channel]. Imagine my surprise when, through my binoculars, I make out her name to be the "Arklow Wind" registered in Arklow, Ireland. What chance that two Irish ships are passing each other in the English Channel! We both waved to each other over a distance of about 100 yards and I took photos of her with my new camera.

At 0915 I was observing a large orange ship on the Starboard bow which seemed to have a boom out to Starboard. She obviously had lifting gear over her transom stern and was showing what looked like two black balls with a diamond between from her Starboard yardarm. This would make her a dredger but she didn't look like a dredger---more like a yacht very smartly kept up. The thought did cross my mind that she could be Trinity House who are responsible for maintaining the buoys and lights around the British coast but I don't know. Her funnel was black with a white square on it with what looked like writing on it but I wasn't steady enough to focus the binoculars properly. Her upper-works were white. Anyway she finished whatever she was doing and steamed off.

At 0945 I sighted three yachts broad on the Starboard beam. My friend in the "Colin Archer" was about half a mile ahead with his big balloon spinnaker making an impressive sight. He didn't seem to me to be gaining much. Indeed it was my impression that whenever the wind got slightly stronger I was gaining on him and when it went really light he drew away. The wind seemed to be fluctuating between Force 2 and Force 3 and Tarla's speed through the water was fluctuating between 4.5 and 5 knots. By 1100 we had made good 11 miles over the ground in the last two hours and are 40 miles from Cherbourg as the crow flies. [8 hours at 5 knots].

At 1130 the Isle of Wight is just disappearing over the horizon. The wind has dropped to Force 1 or 2 and we are rolling and slating. I decided to give it half an hour and if things don't improve start the engine. At 1200 I furled the spinnaker and started the engine running it at 1400 revs. Speed through the water was now 5.2 knots whilst speed over the ground was 4.9. At 1250 a large merchant ship was overtaking me to Starboard. An even bigger ship was crossing my bows (I thought!) from Port. Another huge container ship had already passed ahead of me. At 1255 I observe that another two merchant ships are coming up over the horizon. We are quite obviously in the shipping lanes!

At 1300 I note in the log that despite doing 5 knots through the water we have only made good two miles over the ground in the last hour. Such are the vagaries of the currents in the channel although I accept that the tide had by now turned against me and was pushing me sideways up channel.

At 1305 I altered course to go under the stern of a large merchantman that was crossing my bows. Even though the "Rule of the Road" gave me the right of way I was not going to risk it! At 1320 I was back on course for Cherbourg. At 1330 I concluded that I had probably crossed the Southbound shipping lane and I was being overtaken by a large Bermudan cutter who was obviously under power with both her headsails furled.

At 1400 I had a ceremonial lowering of the British "Red Duster" from the Starboard cross-trees and the hoisting of the French flag in its place. This reminded me that I had purchased this latter flag with my brother Mark and I wondered what he might be doing at this moment in time. Charting the Tarla's position at 1500 showed that we had only made good 3.5 miles in the last hour.

Also at 1500 I sighted a white bird sitting on the sea close off the Port bow. This must have been an omen because I looked up from the bird and sighted land. "Land Ho!" I shouted for the bird's benefit!

At 1600 I altered course 30 Degrees to Port because I was concerned that due to the time that I was taking the tide would turn again and sweep me past the Cherbourg peninsular. As it turned out I got it exactly right and we followed this new course right up to the West fort of Cherbourg harbour!

At 1745 I set the two headsails (The main was already set) and motor-sailed hard on the wind. The "Tarla" was making 6 knots through the water and 6.3 knots over the ground. I wrote in the log "Half a moon has just appeared" even though it was broad day-light. Perhaps it is another omen!

At 1800 I plotted my position on the chart. The tide has not yet turned but it soon will. I wonder how long slack water lasts but I am aiming up-tide of the harbour entrance even though I still have 14 miles to go.

At about this time I identified what I thought were buildings ahead standing out from the background of the land. I couldn't decide whether this was true or was it a huge container ship hull down crossing ahead of me. Eventually it turned out to be the latter because buildings don't move!

At 1830 the tidal arrows on the chart-plotter turned round and from then on speed over the ground was less than speed through the water.

Having plotted my position on the chart every half hour since we left the West Princess buoy I can see that we have travelled on a great loop which is 80 miles long and not 63. The first 6 hours of the ebb tide pushing us down channel while the next six hours moved us up channel which according to my original calculations should have cancelled each other out although with hindsight the flow South proved stronger than the flow North. Now for the last part of the passage the tide was pushing us down channel again.

At 1950 the sun is setting over a blue calm sea and it will be dark in a couple of hours. At 2015 the wind dropped completely and I stowed all three sails. At 2030 because of the tide going past the entrance at 1.6 knots I am aiming at the middle fort in order to enter by the Western one! There are 2.5 miles to go!

At 2105 we passed by the Western Fort of Cherbourg harbour. There is a stupendous sunset and as it is getting dark I switch on the Navigation lights as I motor through the "Grande Rade" and thence into the "Petite Rade" and come to anchor outside the Marina wall at 2145.

5
CHERBOURG TO GUERNSEY

No sooner had I anchored at 2145 outside the Cherbourg Marina on Sunday the 20th of June than disaster struck! I picked up my mobile with a view to sending a text to Niall, Aoife and Anne announcing my safe arrival. There was one very nice message on it from Anne which must have been picked up off the Isle of Wight before I got out of range. The phone suggested, as they do, that I request a network. I did and immediately the screen lit up with "SIMCARD REJECTED" and nothing that I could do would make the phone work again. No contact numbers--- it was as if the phone had locked solid. This is where the modern World hits you! When I was at sea in the early 1960's it could take weeks for a letter to arrive from the far corners of the Earth. Even a telegram saying "Happy Christmas" sent by Morse Code to the Radio Officer on your ship was an expensive business although he had special "Christmassy" telegrams to write it on!

Now I was cut off from instant communication which I had become totally used to. Worse was that if I didn't solve the problem quickly people would start to get worried. I was dead tired. I had had a long day. I went to bed and slept like a log but inside me I was working on the problem. Before retiring I cooked myself something to eat and had a Jameson Whiskey to celebrate having crossed the English Channel.

I had much to celebrate. Tarla had been underway for 17.5 hours. She had covered 83 miles over the ground instead of the 66 in a straight line (an extra 17 miles caused by the tide) at an average speed over the ground of 4.74 knots. Unfortunately, due to the log sticking (although OK when zeroed) I cannot give the total distance through the water which would have made an interesting comparison. During the 17.5 hours she spent only 5.75 hours under sail with the remaining 11.75 hours being under engine (sometimes sail assisted).

Monday the 21st June, 2010. (Midsummer).

Got up at 1100 and had a cup of tea. Changed all the clocks to French time (+ 1 hour). Looked at charts almanac etc trying to decide on strategy for the future. Concluded that I needed to make shorter daily journeys because the tides from now on were going to be much stronger and they only run one way for six hours!

At 1200 I hauled up the anchor and headed into the Marina. The charge for an 8 metre boat (Summer season) was Euro 18 per day with a 20% discount if you belonged to a recognised yacht club. I told them that the only yacht club that I was a member of was the Walton and Frinton Yacht Club but he looked it up on a list and said that it wasn't recognised because they had never applied for recognition. Electricity was free, there was no surcharge for catamarans and showers cost 2 euro and were operated by purchasing "Jetons".

At 1300 I went into Cherbourg searching for someone to sort out my mobile phone which still said "SIMCARD REJECTED". Orange solved the problem by selling me a French Simcard so that my phone now gives me all the instructions in French. I have 20 euro worth of credit which I lose if I don't use it in the next month. At the moment I have no idea how to put more in. No doubt if I go to an Orange shop they will do it for me! With my fully functioning phone I rang Niall, Aoife and Anne and gave them my new French telephone number. Aoife kindly offered to get me a new Simcard with my old number and I told her to put it into one of her spare phones and when my good friend Peter Spry-Leverton, who I was at school with, and is cruising in a Peter Duck Ketch to the South of me rang she would be able to give him my new number. His number, which was wiped from my phone, would then be on her phone and she would be able to let me have it. I also got Niall to send him an e-mail telling him my new number and as a final thought I rang his home in London and left my new number on his answering machine with the thought that his wife might be there, but in fact I think she is in China.

At 1500 I went shopping in the superb Hypermarket. At 1800 I went for a shower. At 1900 I drank a whole bottle of red wine while eating smoked salmon and different French cheeses and fruit. At 2200 I went to bed. Had a phone call from Anne and went to sleep.

Cherbourg is strategically sited. As the peninsular here comes closest to Southern England and its harbour can be entered safely in all weathers it has always been historically important. The massive fortifications were started in Louis XVI's time although they were not finished until 1853. There is now a military port on the West side of the Petite Rade and the ferries at the Eastern end still dock next to the old transatlantic terminal from which the first scheduled service to New York began in 1869. Inside a further breakwater lies the Chantereyne Marina where I am moored, and further in still the Avant Port where yachts used to lie in the heart of the city. Beyond this is the lock-in "Bassin à Flot" where quite large craft can be left safely for extended periods.

The transatlantic terminus building was designed by the architect René Levasseur and was unveiled by the French President Albert Lebrun on the 30th July 1933. This terminus was a bustling hub of activity until the 1960's when the ship-born transatlantic passenger trade collapsed. In December 1989 this building was added to France's list of protected historical buildings and today represents the last surviving example of European maritime architecture. Since April 2002 the building has been home to Cherbourg's maritime museum.

The Vikings arrived in Normandy early in the 10th century and bequeathed their Scandinavian linguistics to the names of many places in the region. Norman toponyms also borrowed from the Celtic language of the pre-Roman Gauls, giving place names a distinct rainbow of etymologies. The tot in "Yvetot" heralds a "rural residence"; the beuf in "Elbeuf" indicates a "house" or "village". Accordingly bec refers to a "waterway" (Claudebec, Bolbec); fleur to an "estuary" or "port"(Honfleur, Barfleur), hou to an island (Tatihou) and homme to a place on the water. Thus a study of the chart allows the local landscape to unfurl before you!

Tuesday the 22nd of June, 2010.

I got up at 0700 and as usual had a cup of tea with some 'shreddies' and at 0830 checked how much fuel I had left in the tank. I was pleasantly surprised to discover that we had used no more than 10 litres for the 11.75 hours of motoring across the channel. I spent all morning writing up Tarla's Log having coffee at 1100 and lunch at 1200.

During this time I was approached by the Marina staff and asked if I would mind shifting berth as "le Vieux Copain" was coming in and would require my berth. I shifted berth and "le Vieux Copain duly arrived and in the usual French fashion moored up. "le Vieux Copain" has an interesting history. Gaff Cutter rigged with jigger mizzen, what I would call a Gaff yawl, she was built in les Sables d'Olonnes at the Espoirs boatyard and launched in 1940 during the war. She was the pride and joy of Gaston Poiraud, a native of the Île d'Yeu, until he gave up fishing for tuna in 1974. After this "le Vieux Copain" took part in an expedition to Greenland which was organised by an association from Grenoble but unfortunately ran aground in the Orkney Islands. After making makeshift repairs she was written off by the insurance company and towed to Paimpol by her new owner. He then lived on her for a year before selling her on. In new ownership she was subject to further neglect and a storm keeled her over in the mud of Coz-Castel, where she remained partially submerged destined for eventual disintegration with no hope of ever seeing Brehat or the Phare de la Croix ever again.

In May 1983, the wreck was bought by Serge Le Joliff who set about restoring her. Finally, in 1989, after some 9000 hours of hard work, "le Vieux Copain" took her place on the waters as the pride of Paimpol. (You can see her on www.voiles-ecarlates.fr)

At 1430 I went to the Chandlery to purchase a "Q" flag (yellow flag) as I had discovered from the "pilot" that I would have to clear through customs when I visited Guernsey which was my next port of call. This is despite Guernsey being British and part of the EU. In my youth this was standard procedure when visiting a foreign country but with the opening up of the borders of the EU countries it is now rarely required within Europe if one comes from another European Country. Needless to say the one flag that they had sold out of was the "Q" flag. There was also a requirement that I should present a completed customs form upon arrival (Part 1 of form C1328) and I didn't have one. On the other hand, I could remember visiting Guernsey with my friend Peter Spry-Leverton in his Peter Duck Ketch about 10 years ago and we had the same problem of no "Q" flag and no custom's form and they didn't put us in prison so I decided to risk it!

At 1500 I put together the shopping trolley, with fold down seat for geriatrics, which my sister Rachel and her husband had very kindly bought me and set off for the Hypermarket half a mile away. I bought 6 bottles of wine and lots of stores and I could hardly lift the trolley off the ground! None of the wine cost me more than 4 euro a bottle and would have been at least three times as expensive in Cork.

At 1700 I went and filled up my 10 litre can with Diesel putting it in the shopping trolley to transport it. (Cost 12 Euro 10 for 10 litres). I filled up the Tarla's main fuel tank to the brim and then went back and filled my 10 litre can again so as to hold it in reserve.

At 2000 I went for a shower and at 2030 had a pleasant meal in the cockpit of Salad, Bread, and Cheese having started with smoked salmon! At 2100 I answered e-mails and made out my passage plan for Guernsey and after a couple of whiskeys went to bed at 2230.

Passage planning on the French coast from now on becomes increasingly challenging. Most of the coast is rocky. There are many off-lying dangers. There can be fog and bad weather and there are very strong currents which at or near spring tides can reach rates of up to 10 knots even when the tidal diamonds on the chart only say 5! With a strong wind over tide the sea becomes like a cauldron and few small boats survive.

My passage plan from Cherbourg to Guernsey took me through the race of Alderney which is one of these challenging spots. I had to arrive at the race half an hour before HW Dover. As HW Dover was at 1030 French time I would have to leave Cherbourg at about 0700. It was 10 miles from the Western Fort to Cap de la Hague and another 5 miles until I would be halfway between Cap de la Hague and Alderney and could turn and go through the race. I intended to approach St. Peter Port, Guernsey through the Little Russel which has many rocks to catch the unwary. On the way I would have to avoid "la Banc de la Schôle" as it is notorious for kicking up a vicious sea. I needed clear visibility and not too much wind and the "Meteo" report pinned up in the Harbour office seemed to promise these conditions for the morrow. The total distance over the ground to be covered from Cherbourg to Guernsey was 42.7 miles.

Wednesday 28th June, 2010.

0600 Got up and prepared the "Tarla" for the trip. 0700 cast off from the pontoon in Cherbourg Marina. 0730 Cherbourg Western Fort in the harbour entrance abeam. Streamed log (set at zero) Engine 1400 revs. Speed through the water 5.3 knots. Speed over the ground 4.8 knots. Course 300 deg. True. Distance to run on this course 10 miles. It is a beautiful sunny morning. Flat calm and the sea is like a mirror.

At 0800 I was threading my way between fisherman's buoys with the log recording 2.27. The land we are passing about one mile away is very green and rich with the houses sparkling in the sun. At 0815 CH1 buoy is abeam to Starboard and I am being overtaken by a large Belgian sloop motor-sailing with her mainsail up (not much point in the latter as there is absolutely no wind). There are 2 yachts out ahead of me and 2 coming up astern all going the same way as me towards the Alderney race. I presume that we have all done the same tidal calculations!

0830 Course 300 deg. True. Log 5.28 miles through the water since the Western Fort. The Stowe trailing log agrees with the "Tack Tick" speedometer!

0900 Log 7.70. Course 300 deg. True. Basse Bréfort North Cardinal Buoy is broad on the Port bow.

0917 Basse Bréfort abeam to Port. Log 9.10. Speed through the water 5.1 knots. Speed over the ground 6.8 knots. The back eddy close to the shore is now helping us although the tide has yet to turn at the Alderney race. Cap de la Hague is now broad on the Port bow. Alderney is in sight in the distance and "la Plate", which we have to give a wide berth to, is also in sight off the Port bow.

0928 Log 10.00. Altered course to 270 deg. True. Distance to run on this course 5 miles. Way out to sea to Starboard I can see a Ferry making for Cherbourg. To Port I am being overtaken by a British Southerly yacht which I think was the one moored close to me in Cherbourg. We are making 5 knots through the water and 7.5 knots over the ground. I am keeping to Starboard of my track now steering 279 (Degrees True) "Playing Safe" and the Southerly is crossing ahead of me. Alderney is now very clear on the horizon.

0943 "La Plate" is abeam of me to Port. Speed through the water 4.8 knots and speed over the ground 7.8 knots. Log 11.12 Wind WNW Force 1 on the nose. There is a superb lighthouse on the end of Cap de la Hague and I took a photo. At 0948 this lighthouse was abeam. Speed through the water 4.5 knots. Speed over the ground 8.2 knots. Log 11.54 miles. Altered course to 275 deg. True. I am heading directly for the lighthouse on the up-channel end of Alderney and the race is to Port of me.

10000 Log 12.42. Speed through the water 5 knots. Speed over the ground 6.7 knots. Course 261 Deg. True. As it is now half an hour before HW Dover the tide should now be slack. I am still heading for the lighthouse on the up-channel end of Alderney. It has a black and white striped tower and a winking light.

1030 Altered course to 230 deg. True. Log 15.00 Speed through the water 5 knots. Speed over the ground 6.4 knots. We are now in the race of Alderney!

The Island of Alderney is passing by to Starboard. It looks like a large outcrop of rock with a green table-cloth on it. There is, however, one small yellow patch high up in the centre which is probably a field of Barley or some such crop. There are few houses to be seen as the harbour and main settlement are on the other side and I understand that about 2000 people live there permenently with many more coming in the summer. The huge rocks sticking out of the water at the down-channel end are like big teeth or fangs which give one a feeling of foreboding. What must they look like in a great storm?

1100 Log 17.35. Speed through the water 4.9 knots. Speed over the ground 8.2 knots. Course 222 deg. True. I am now being overtaken by a large cruise liner! I am also converging with a yacht which is abeam to Port. Another yacht behind me is overtaking. I have now noticed two very large cream painted buildings on the edge of the cliffs about two miles away. Probably Hotels! There are great swirls in the water as we make good 8 knots over the ground. These are presumably great up-wellings from the uneven bottom which is currently 44.7 metres deep.

11.15 Guernsey in sight ahead (Just). Jersey is very clear away to the South. It looks to be much higher land. (This turned out to be false!)

1130 The rocks at the end of Alderney are now abeam to Starboard. I am being overtaken by an UKSA sailing sloop with mainsail set and a black cone, point downwards, showing that she is motor-sailing. I made a cup of tea and had a nice chunk of Anne's cake. The log reads 19.58. The Course is 235 deg. True. The speed through the water is 4.9 knots and the speed over the ground is 7.6 knots.

1145 I am between Alderney and "La Banc de la Schôle". I am on course for "la Plate Fougère" off Guernsey. Distance 19.90. The log reads 20.86. it is now very warm and I am only wearing shirt and trousers, socks and shoes. The temperature is 17.6 deg. C. And the humidity 73%. The sky is hazy and hot. The Casquets lighthouse is abeam to Starboard---a most impressive feat of engineering built, as it is, on a rock which sticks out of the sea. It is still winking its light despite the bright sunshine!

1200 Altered course to 230 deg. True. Log 22.00. Speed through the water 5kns. 1400 revs. Speed over the ground 6.7 knots.

My earlier identification of Jersey was obviously wrong! It was the island of Sark which is now clearly visible with Herm in between it and Guernsey.

1230 Put position on the chart as I do each half hour or hour. There is a very small container ship passing to Starboard going the other way. Obviously he is not working his tides! He has 6 containers end to end which fill his deck lengthwise and I cannot see how many he has side by side. I look him up on

AIS and discover that he is making 8.6 knots over the ground and although he has an MMSI number the space for the ship's name is blank!

1300 "La Platte Fougère" off Guernsey is 4.5 miles away according to the chart-plotter. The log reads 27.15. Speed through the water is 5 knots. The engine revs are 1400.

1315 "La Platte Fougère" is in sight with its black and white stripes and we are heading straight for it.

1345 After a lot of internal debate concerning which buoy was which and the correct answer mattered as the channel here is strewn with rocks many of which are just under the surface I clearly identified the buoy called Roustal and altered course. By altering course and keeping this buoy in line with Brehon any side drift caused by the current could be controlled---that is the beauty of transits. The log read 31.00.

At 1403 Roustal was close abeam to Port. Log 32.61. Speed over the ground 6.7 knots. I hauled the log and altered course to 220 deg. True for St Peter Port harbour. A small cruise ship called "The Discovery" was anchored just off the harbour entrance. I rigged mooring lines and fenders on both sides and slowed to 3 knots to let a motor lighter with some containers on deck enter harbour before me.

At 1500 I entered harbour and at 1515 tied up to another boat rafted alongside a pontoon. A man in a motor launch handed me a customs form to fill in and when he returned I handed it to him. I paid £18 for a night on a pontoon berth in the middle of the harbour and after a lot of shifting around ended up moored next to the "Iseult" a very beautiful gaff yawl which has appeared in the magazines "Classic Boat Owner" and "Yachting Monthly" as she was 100 years old in 2009. Her owner told me that he and his wife purchased her in 1964 and have been sailing her ever since with little to do but odd maintenance jobs each year.

Opposite me on the pontoon was a powerful Belgian sloop with four old men on her. They had set out for the Azores but had put in here because of lack of wind. One can hardly blame them for not wanting to motor all the way to the Azores! Nevertheless, they appeared to have enough Diesel as they had many 20 litre drums lashed on deck!

The third interesting vessel close by was a small 8 metre junk-rigged craft with two old men on her. Her name was the "*Hui Mar*" and she had Chinese writing on the back of what was obviously a Western hull-form.

I had cheese, pâté, beer and wine and went for a snooze from 1600 to 2000. Then I cooked baked beans mixed with sardines, had two whiskeys and two glasses of red wine and turned in at 2300hrs.

Guernsey is the seat of government of the Bailiwick of Guernsey, which includes Alderney, Jethou, Herm and Sark. The permanent population number some 55,000 with an additional half a million tourists arriving in the summer season. These tourists are attracted by romantic notions of island life and the duty free shopping (Guernsey has no VAT). As a result of being geared up to tourism the main thrust seems to be the advertising of amenities and the true Guernsey, what lies beneath stemming from its unique history, tends to get lost. The 800 year old Castle Cornet would have many stories to tell! Unfortunately, given my desire to get to Southern Brittany, I was not in a position to linger.

The other thing that Guernsey evoked in me was the many stories told by British yachtsmen of visiting over the years. As a direct result of the very large differences between high and low water quite deep yachts could be put up against the harbour wall and have their bottoms scrubbed and new anti-fouling paint applied between tides. The names of Eric Hiscock and Roger Pinkney and the beautiful yacht "Dyarchy" come to mind. One of the pioneers of cruising in small yachts for pleasure who even pre-dated Claude Worth (who wrote his books on "Cruising" before the First World War) was McMullan who describes in his book "Down Channel" paying off his two paid crew in the Channel Islands (because of their feckless nature) and sailing his very large and heavy English Gaff Cutter back up channel on his own. One of the more interesting facts about him is that he makes no mention of Mrs. McMullan in his book even though I have it from reliable sources that she was aboard. Presumably he did not mention her because she took no part in the sailing of the vessel. The thing that I admire about McMullan is that he applied the highest professional standards to the pursuit of yachting a fact which Claude Worth and many others have paid tribute to.

6
GUERNSEY
TO TRÉGUIER

Thursday 24ᵗʰ June, 2010

0700 Got up. Had a cup of tea and prepared a passage plan.

0900 I cast off from the pontoon in St Peter Port bound for Tréguier in Northern Brittany. As I came out of the harbour entrance I noticed a vast Cruise liner anchored and running her passengers ashore in her motor-boats. The "Discovery" of yesterday had gone! I took a photo.

0910 Streamed log (zeroed). Set the mainsail and stopped the engine. Set both headsails. Making 3 knots through the water and over the ground.

0925 This is gorgeous slipping along at 4 knots in a force 2 NW wind.

0955 St. Martin's White Tower Lighthouse Abeam to Starboard. Log 2.14. Altered course to 220 deg. True. Speed through the water 2.8 knots. Speed over the ground 3.2 knots. The back-eddy is helping us!

I should explain that the tidal pattern between Guernsey and Northern Brittany, although strong, is not much help. Of the 6 hours of what you might think would be fair tide only about two hours of it is helping you on your way, the rest is moving you sideways. As you approach Northern Brittany the foul tide will be flowing against you as it comes round the corner. By starting with the tide against me and making use of the back-eddy flowing South from St. Peter Port I hoped to maximise my chances although I suspected that I would be lucky to break even by the end of the day. As always, it would depend how long the passage took me.

1000 The wind has suddenly gone round to the South! Force 1 to 2. Speed through the water 2.9 knots. Speed over the ground 4.7 knots. Course 230 deg. True.

1010 Started the engine! Furled headsails. Revs 1400. Speed through the water had dropped to 2.3 knots and Tarla would only lay a course of 238 deg. True. With the engine running I put her back on a course of 220 deg. True. She was now making 5.3 knots through the water and 6.5 knots over the ground. The brief Southerly wind then died away to a mirror like calm.

1025 The wind is now coming from the North East which is on the beam. I reduced engine revs to 1000 and reset the staysail and jib. Speed through the water 4.9 knots and speed over the ground 5.3. Log 4.02. The sea has a definite swell to it for the first time since this voyage began and the water has tiny ripples on it made by the light wind. The swell is very much influenced by the proximity to the Atlantic. Sailing out of Cork harbour one would almost always have it. Sailing out of the Walton backwaters one would hardly ever get it. It strikes me in passing that Thames sailing barges and fishing smacks hardly ever had to operate in swell.

1230 Furled jib. The rolling in the swell keeps putting it "aback" as there is not enough wind to fill it. The main-boom is also swinging from side to side too! I am trying to read my book!

1250 Passed through long lines of a white substance on the surface of the sea as well as passing lots of plastic bags and other rubbish. I wonder what the white substance is?

There is a huge lighthouse clearly visible broad on the Port bow. This is Roches Douvres Light House and it is certainly very impressive! It is 5 miles away according to the chart-plotter and is supposed to be green although I cannot confirm that from this distance even with the binoculars. But then earlier I thought that it was the sail of a yacht! The tide is still pushing me away from it so I should be O.K. You can see the low lying rocks which extend up to one and a half miles from it with the swell breaking on them. Otherwise it is just a lighthouse sitting in the middle of the sea!

At 1320 I increased engine revs to 1400. Speed through the water 5.5 knots. Speed over the ground 5.6 knots. The tide will shortly be turning against us and we still have 20 miles to go! There is a large fishing boat in sight off my Port bow and at 1335 it crosses ahead of me. At 1350 I furled the staysail and sheeted the mainsail in hard. We are back to a flat calm with a rolling swell.

1430 Furled the main-sail.

1530 Land Ho! Broad on the Port beam. At 1538 a fast motor yacht crossed my bows heading North. At 1520 a large aluminium French sailing yacht with two furled headsails under mainsail and engine passed me to Port. I have rigged my Starboard sunshade and it works! I am reading my book but I am amazed at how many small black flies can be so far out to sea. They are an awful nuisance as one has to keep swatting them off.

1600 Log 31.73. Course 230 (T). Speed through the water 5.3 knots. Revs 1400. Speed over the ground 4.0 knots. Put position on chart. 4.2 miles made good in last hour. The tide has turned!

1730 A large Merchant Ship is crossing astern at an oblique angle obviously bound South. A yacht motor-sailing has crossed ahead in the distance probably going to Tréguier. Plotted position on the chart. Have made good 1.4 miles in the last half hour. At 1740 I sighted Jument Buoy to Port.

1820 Jument Buoy abeam to Port. Merchant Ship overtaking me to Starboard (about 4 miles further out in the channel).

1850 Crublent Buoy in sight and the Green and Red Buoys of the channel in towards Tréguier identified. This identification is vital as we are surrounded by rocks and the tide sweeps one sideways so buoys and transits become all important.

1910 Crublent Buoy abeam to Port. Log 47.98. This Buoy marks the outer end of the channel into Tréguier and is notoriously difficult to identify from the sea. Jument which is nearby is easier but you still have to be quite close to see it. At night, of course, they would be much easier to see because of their lights.

At 2000 La Corne marker is abeam to Port. Log 52.13 and I then continued a further 4 miles up the river and anchored in 5.5 metres below the Château that Tom Cunliffe (who wrote my pilot book) rode out Hurricane Charlie in his boat in 1986. There is a picture of the Château in the pilot book so I know I was in the right place.

Had two glasses of wine, eat cheese, pâté and biscuits, a banana and finished off the cherries, filled and lit the paraffin riding light and turned in at 2300 having sent my usual text messages.

7
TRÉGUIER
TO TRÉBEURDEN

After dropping the anchor in 5.5 metres I had to work out how much the water level would go up and down from there otherwise I might find that I was either aground at low water or floated up so high that the anchor would no longer be touching the bottom! By consulting the tide tables I established that at Mean High Water Springs Tréguier had a tidal range of 8 metres and at Mean High Water Neaps a range of 4.2 metres. As we were coming up to Springs I assumed the former. I had anchored at approximately half tide in 5.5 metres. Therefore my boat would rise another 4 metres and at low tide would drop 4 metres. Thus the water under my keel (I draw less than one metre) would range from 0.5 metres approx (5.5 − 4.0 less the 1 metre that Tarla draws) to 8.5 metres (5.5 + 4.0 less 1). As it is recommended that you put out at least three times the chain at the greatest depth I put out 30 metres. The interested reader will already have appreciated that as the tide turns the swinging room will be much greater at low water than at high. Fortunately for me there was nobody else anchored there so it didn't matter!

Friday the 25th of June, 2010.
At 0500 I got up briefly to check the anchor and riding light. Paraffin lamps have a habit of blowing out. However, everything was fine and it was a beautiful calm night. At 0900 I got up again

and had my usual cup of tea and worked on typing up the log on my computer. By 1800 I had finished and during this long typing session I sustained myself on cups of coffee and Anne's cake and 2 pints of beer for lunch.

I am now in the land of the Celts just like when I am in Ireland. Brittany, or the Amorican peninsula as it was known in antiquity, is famed for its numerous Neolithic monuments. Most of the great burial chambers here predate the Egyptian pyramids by a long time. They consisted of dolmen, or stone chambers, for the bodies, covered by a tumulus, an earth mound. There are countless Neolithic menhirs, or standing stones, which excite academic debate even to this day.

Brittany's history becomes much less clear in the long gap between the Neolithic period and the arrival of the Romans. Prior to Caesar's conquest of Armorica in the Iron Age a strong Celtic culture emerged and although little has survived the notion of the druids embedded in the mists of time still lives on.

During the dark ages, wave upon wave of immigrants from Ireland, Wales and Southern England swept into the Amorican peninsular and created "Little Britain" or Brittany. They spread their own brand of Christianity as well as their exuberant legends and a feisty independent Brittany was thus formed.

After the Breton Kingdom came the Breton Duchy. First harassed by the Vikings, the region's leaders also had to contend with powerful neighbours. A bitter Breton civil war thus broke out in the 14th Century with Franco Breton and Anglo Breton factions. Forts sprang up and the towns were protected behind strong walls. New gothic cathedrals were built in the cities.

Major changes occurred in Brittany as the 15th Century became the 16th. Gothic styles of architecture gave way to those of the Renaissance. The feisty duchy lost its independence to the French crown while at the same time Breton traders led the way in international commerce and organised vast fishing expeditions to Newfoundland. It is even claimed that Jacques

Cartier discovered America!

In the 17th and 18th centuries the French Monarchy imposed its iron will on Brittany and the Breton people, their language and culture became subservient to the will of Paris. This 'iron will' and the repression that went with it led to the revolution but the conservative Bretons took little part in it. Nevertheless, as a centre for trade and colonial expansion this region was very important to France and the conservative Bretons joined the French Navy and fought against the British.

During the 19th Century Breton industry developed but there were large numbers of very poor people involved in agriculture and fishing who suffered from near starvation. This poverty was only alleviated during the second half of the 20th century after Brittany recovered from the devastation caused by the German occupation of the Second World War and France had joined the European Economic Community. Today, Brittany is one of France's major tourist destinations and the local economy has benefitted accordingly.

At 2018 I was passed by a boat being steered by an oar with a small lateen sail with a girl trying to relieve herself over the side keeping the sail between me and her! There were two girls and one boy on the boat. I took a photo but made sure that the girl was hidden behind the sail!

2100 Had supper of baked beans and sausages. Finished off the grapes which had been purchased in Cherbourg. Drank 2 glasses of red wine. Had a whiskey. Read my book and at 2300 went to bed.

At 2400 I was woken by Anne phoning and had a wonderful talk. It was so good to hear her voice.

Saturday 26th of June, 2010.

At 0430 I was woken by a motorboat going past although in general this was a very peaceful well sheltered anchorage. It was a beautiful calm night with the stars twinkling. I made myself a cup of tea and read my book and at 0530 went back to bed again.

0830 I got up again and had breakfast. Did the washing up and rigged fenders and mooring ropes both sides. At 0945 I started the engine, hauled up the anchor and proceeded about half a mile round a bend in the river to the Tréguier marina where I tied up at 1015. The tide was running against me at half a knot and this determined my choice of finger berth as I obviously wanted to approach up-tide. I went to the Capitanerie and paid Euro 21.20 which included two free showers and free electricity for 24 hours. There was no surcharge for catamarans. After this I went shopping and had great difficulty finding a supermarket amongst all the ancient buildings and tourist shops but eventually succeeded by following an old lady with a shopping trolley!

The town of Tréguier is a medieval town with many of its original buildings. It features a remarkable and ancient cathedral called " La Cathedrale Saint Tugdual" with a bizarre spire which although ascending to a point has many holes in it. Louis XVI paid for the clock. This place of worship contains the tomb of St Yves who is the patron saint of lawyers (and as a sideline also of the poor!). Every May there is a procession in his honour involving many people. As a likeness of St Yves lies on top of his tomb in the middle of the Cathedral [with an ornate stone canopy over him] I was able to photograph him from a number of different angles with my new camera. Ernest Renan, the great Philologist, lived for the first 15 years of his life in a fine 17th Century wood panelled house which the public can visit and there is also an impressive statue of Ernest Renan and Athena. Ernest was born in 1823. Constructed in the 17th Century the Augustinian Convent is also notable. The Augustinian Sisters arrived in Tréguier in 1654 and provided refuge for the poor. The Megaliths of Tossen Keller are also worth seeing, They were discovered in Penevenan and now reside on the Tréguier Quays.

They are arranged as 58 rocks in the shape of an ellipse open at its Eastern end.

1300 Had lunch. Discovered that one of my left upper teeth had broken off after biting into a baguette. This left a jagged root. Luckily it is not as jagged as previous teeth that have done this. (This is the 6th tooth to do this in the last 7 years and the Dentist just rebuilds them but it will have to wait until I get back to Cork).

1400 went for a snooze and at 1500 for a shower and Anne rang me which was very nice.

At 1600 I rang Niall as I appeared to be getting WIFI in the marina. Discovered that the NETABORD network had to be paid for and that Niall was not allowed to sign me up for it in Ireland. It can only be done by a person using a credit card in France. This was beyond me! The dongle which I used so successfully in England is put on a very high roaming rate in France and hence all your credit goes in the briefest of time!

Between 1730 and 1830 I did some more typing and then had a glass of wine and started reading Michael Harrington's book which he had presented me with in Eastbourne. It was a beautiful Summer evening as I sat in the cockpit but fog was forecast for the morrow so I felt that I should sit tight. I made myself a meal and eat it.

At 1940 I made contact with my friend Peter Spry-Leverton at last. He phoned me after my daughter Aoife who had put my replacement Simcard into one of her phones in Cork had picked up his number when he rang. Aoife then contacted me and rang him to give him my new French number. Peter was anchored in his Peter Duck Ketch in the Îles de Glénan bound North. We decided to contact each other in a couple of days and see where we could meet up.

At 2200 I went to bed and Anne phoned after that but something happened and we were cut off.

Sunday the 27ᵗʰ of June, 2010.

0700 Got up and there was a thick fog as forecast! You could hardly see to the end of the pontoon and so I did some more typing. At 1000 hrs I went to the Capitanerie, which according to the notice on the door should have been open from 0900 to 1100. I stood around outside with a number of Brits who all wanted to pay and nobody turned up. The fog had now gone--- burnt up by the sun like a morning mist.

One of the Brits was a chap with a Steadfast Motor-Sailor some 24 feet long. He had been cruising in this area for many years and did not like paying for Marinas so he usually anchored somewhere. His homeport was Southampton from where he always started his cruise each Summer and where he always completed it. His wife was dead and his daughter had married a Breton---hence his interest in coming to Brittany each Summer. His daughter and her family would be joining him that afternoon. He reckoned that he used half a gallon of Diesel per hour and that it would take him ten hours to reach Guernsey from Tréguier. He certainly knows his anchorages and has cruised for weeks at a time round this coast and through the Breton canals. He was once an electrician in the Merchant Navy sailing with Bank Line for 5 years in the early 1960's.

1100 Returned to Tarla for coffee.

1200 Went Shopping. Bought more tins, strawberries and cheese. Purchased one of the last baguettes in the Cathedral square.

1300 Had lunch. Drank a pint of beer and had a snooze until 1500 when I resumed typing until 1800hrs. I then made out a passage plan to Trébeurden and onwards to L'AberWrac'h.

1840 poured myself a glass of red wine.

1940 Just checked the main fuel tank---it is only half full. Must have used 30 litres from Cherbourg to Tréguier in 18 1/2 hours motoring at 1400 revs which equates to almost 1 ½ litres per hour. Here on the pontoon Tarla appears to be going backwards at a rate of knots even though she is tied up. This is caused by the flow of water moving past caused by the spring tides.

I love the way that the Vion weather station in Tarla's cabin (which is French) tells me whether I am comfortable or not. At the moment it says that I am. Currently, the temperature inside the cabin and outside in the cockpit is exactly the same 21.9 degrees Celsius. The humidity in the cabin is higher than in the cockpit 69% as against 62% outside. The weather station shows a symbol with both the sun and a cloud on it but looking outside I would describe it as hazy sunshine. The clock is radio controlled from Paris and can only give you French time which is very useful here but less useful in England where I purchased it. Although it is French it tells you that you are comfortable or wet etc in English so at this moment in time it has COMFORT written on the screen. My French/English Dictionary (albeit a small one) does not list this as a French word!

2230 I have just had a lengthy discussion with a chap that owns a Vancouver 34 Pilot House Cutter about the problems in England. His view is that they arise as a result of the English class structure which still lives on. The French "Enthusiast" who has worked all day, and all day yesterday, in his shorts on his boat which is called "Fine a l'eau" is still at it despite the fact that it is getting dark.

2300 turned in.

Monday 28th of June, 2010.

I was woken at 0600 by an awful noise like a fishing line running out and then snapping. After considerable research I discovered that the very strong current moving past Tarla, as if she were going backwards at a rate of knots, had suddenly forced the rudders over. The rudders were constrained by the autopilot belt which was locked. However, the force was such that the belt had slipped and this had made the noise which I had heard. Fortunately, no harm had been done.

0630 had a cup of tea and at 0645 fog suddenly moved in. My hopes were that it was an early morning mist which would be burnt off by the sun as it was yesterday. We had had no update on the "Meteo" because no one turned up to open the Capitanerie yesterday. Anyway I decided to get ready to go. I could always reverse my decision later. I proposed to consult the harbourmaster when at 0800 he, hopefully, would turn up.

0730 Went up into the town looking for a "Tabac" to purchase Euro 15 credit for my French phone. This I did but I couldn't understand the French instructions as to how to put it in!

0800 Reported to the Capitaneric and the Harbour Master was full of apologies for the fact that his colleague had not turned up on the previous day. I got him to put the credit into my phone but he did it so quickly that I was still none the wiser! I paid for berthing on Sunday (E21.20); 10 litres of Diesel (E11.20) and at 0840 cast off from the pontoon. The mist was clearing and the sun was coming out. At 0857 I passed the Château where I had previously anchored and with revs set at 1000 and speed through the water and speed over the ground of 4.3 knots I proceeded down river. The tide would soon turn in my favour and there was another yacht going down ahead of me.

At 0958 La Corne was abeam.

1015 Rounded Pen ar Guezec.

1039 Basse Crublent Buoy abeam. I was now out at sea again. I streamed the log (zeroed), set the course of 258(T). Distance 17 miles to a position chosen by me off Bar-ar-Gall West Cardinal Buoy.

1045 I am being thrown about by the swell and the uneven bottom of the sea which causes "upwelling". You can see the swells breaking on the rocks away to port and there are 3 yachts up ahead of me going the same way. At 1105 an American yacht passed me going the other way and at 1110 a ketch with her mainsail set passed me to Port doing likewise. It is hazy out here but you can still see the land.

1115 a huge lump of rock has appeared out of the haze on the Starboard bow. This must be one of the Sept Isles. We are going to pass between them and the mainland. Two yachts motor-sailing are on a converging course to Starboard. To Port you can see about 2 miles away rows of rocks rising out of the sea. It is now not quite as bumpy as it was off Crublent and this is probably because the water is much deeper. The "Tarla", however, is still rising and falling to the Atlantic swell. The depth of the water here is 50.7 metres. The air temperature is 18.3 degrees Celsius. And the Humidity is 81%.

In the late medieval period monks tried to establish a foothold on the Île aux Moines which is one of Les Sept Isles, but failed. These islands have been described as so many whales lurking out to sea and it was the hunting of Puffins to near extinction on Les Sept Isles that caused the society of the "Ligue pour la Protection des Oiseaux" to be set up in the early part of the 20th century. A puffin is still the emblem of their association.

Puffins are not the only seabird to be found here, the archipelago attracts a phenomenal number of birds that otherwise rarely nest in France. From March through to September one side of the Île Rouzic turns white as snow with the sheer density of the gannets that gather to reproduce. It is the only place that these splendid marine birds nest in France.

The Puffins stay for a shorter period---from March to July normally. Guillemots, fulmars, kittiwakes and Manx shearwaters count among the many other species that thrive here. There is also a small colony of grey seals living amongst the birds.

1130 I plotted my position on the chart as I do every hour or half hour and as a result altered course 5 deg to Starboard to get us back onto track. "Tarla" has made good 3 miles over the ground in the last half hour. The sea is now like a mirror---flat calm. The swell is still a bit bumpy but much better than it was before. I am overtaking a ketch on my Port beam. She has her main and mizzen sails set although she is motor-sailing. Her sails are red like mine! I made a cup of tea and had the penultimate slice of Anne's cake. I am saving the last slice for the trip to L'AberWrac'h when we will pass the 400 mile line from Walton-on-Naze where I started.

1150 The Islands to Starboard are now becoming clearer. I can see four big ones and two little ones which only leaves one missing out of the Sept Isles! One of the big ones has a large lighthouse on it. I am now entering an area where there are rocks on both sides of me but the scenery is stupendous.

1210 Speed over the ground now 7 knots! Altered course another 5 deg to Port to try and bring her back on track. There is a yacht with mainsail up on a converging course to Starboard and another yacht is overtaking me.

1215 The Contessa 32 which I have been following has now set her headsail and stopped her engine so I am overtaking her quickly now. There is still very little wind.

1220 Yellow South Cardinal Buoy abeam to Starboard about 1/4 mile away. Speed through the water 4.7 knots. Speed over the ground 7.1 knots Eng Revs 1400. Log 6.88. Have now overtaken the Contessa.

1230 The lighthouse on the Île Aux Moines is now abeam to Starboard. Log 7.40. I put Tarla head to the wind and hoisted the mainsail. I stopped the engine and set the jib and staysail. Speed through the water 2.5 knots hard on the wind. Speed over the ground 5.1 knots. Tarla made good 7 miles in the last hour. So we are now sailing between Les Sept Isles and the mainland!

1300 Waves are breaking around me as we are passing over a shallow spot. Wind is NW Force 2. "Tarla" is being slowed down by all the bouncing around caused by the "upwelling". Made good 2 miles in the last half hour. Course 260 (T). Bar-ar-Gall is 2.3 miles ahead as measured by the chart-plotter and 2.8 miles as measured from our plotted position on the chart. Given the small scale of the chart and the fact that the chart-plotter may be using a different chart datum I am not surprised at the error.

1315 A yacht passed me on the Port side going the other way. He is certainly battling a foul tide. Bar-ar-Gall Buoy is now in sight off the Port Bow. Altered course so as to clear the buoy comfortably but not be swept past by the tide. 1325 I am being tossed around by a lumpy sea and speed through the water has fallen to 0.8 knots. She just cannot get going!

1340 Bar-ar-Gall Buoy abeam to Port. Log 8.96. Altered course to 215 (T) for Le Crapaud West cardinal Buoy. Course 215 (T) Distance 5 miles.

1430 Log 9.57. Started engine at 1000 revs. Motor-sailing with all three sails up at 4.8 knots through the water (5.4 over the ground). Altered course to 235 (T) and le Crapaud Buoy is in sight on the Port Bow.

Tarla motor-sails very well in these conditions. With the engine at 1000 revs she is now making 5.2 knots through the water due to a slight increase in wind. Say Force 2 which is on the Starboard beam.

1450 Le Crapaud West cardinal Buoy is abeam to Port. Altered course to 200 (T). Log 11.00 miles.

1600 Ar Gouredec Buoy abeam to Port. Handed Log reading 16.16. Furled headsails and lowered mainsail.

1625 Rigged mooring lines and fenders both sides and tied up to a waiting buoy in Trébeurden Harbour. This is because there was not enough water over the sill in the protected harbour for me to get in. I enjoyed a beer in the cockpit while waiting in the sunshine for the tide to rise.

1650 Sometimes yachting fulfils all ones expectations. Out here on the waiting buoy with the sun beating down and one yacht after another coming in and picking up a waiting buoy is one of them.

1715 Started engine. Let go waiting buoy and proceeded into the harbour over the sill. I paid the man E23 for one night's stay plus E1 for a jeton to have a shower. Total 24 euro with again no surcharge for catamarans.

1940 I am sitting here in the cockpit with the sunshade rigged on this loverly sunny evening listening to the group of French men and women chatting away on the yacht next to me. I have just had supper of bread and salami, bread and goat's cheese and lots of cherries. I have decided that I am not going to drink more than ½ a bottle of red wine a night from now on because it is not doing me any good by drinking more.

Trébeurden is an up-market resort featuring 3 star hotels and an 18-hole golf course. This is a highly popular holiday destination for the French who come to this part of Brittany to take part in pony-trekking, surfing and camping amongst the pine trees. Trébeurden's relatively new marina, with sill, provides a safe haven with reasonable tidal access on a part of the coast where there are relatively few alternatives.

2030 Spoke to Niall by phone and at some length and finally managed to access the free internet in the Marina with his help. Probably the only Marina with free internet access on the French coast!

2130 went for a shower.

2215 I am sitting here in the cockpit with a glass of whiskey in my hand watching as the sun goes down over the rocks sticking up out of the sea. An unforgettable sight. This may be a dangerous coast but it is so beautiful.

2300 Turned in.

The Contessa 32 which we were in company with today comes from Lowestoft. Her owner came round to see me after the "Tarla" had been docked. He wanted to discuss our relative speeds under sail. He thought that the "Tarla" was the faster and I most definitely felt that it was the Contessa 32. It didn't strike me until afterwards that what he was referring to was when I had all three sails up AND the engine running at 1000 revs! He was a long way from home and would have to start going back soon. He told me that his wife was insisting that they stay in Trébeurden for at least 3 days and she wanted to be taken out to dinner each night ! I told him that I thought that the Contessa 32 was one of the prettiest of modern yachts, which she is.

The "Blanik" is the name of the Vancouver 34 Pilothouse version that was in Tréguier and that has moved round to Trébeurden with me today. According to her owner she was built in 2002 and although registered in Portsmouth she is moored in Plymouth at a cost of £3,500 a year. Her fridge didn't work for the first 3 years because it was installed with a wire that was too thin that caused "voltage drop". The fridge was a modern "intelligent" fridge and was designed to stop working if the voltage dropped below a certain level and thus would not drain the ship's batteries completely. Thus as it did not receive a high enough voltage it did not work!

The chap I talked to with the 24 foot Steadfast Motor-Sailor told me this morning that he was sailing for Guernsey and that he had worked out the tidal vectors and that over a ten hour passage they would all cancel each other out. I hope they have because he should be there by now. He was filling up with Diesel when I left and given the lack of wind today I reckon he needed it. He informed me that his new partner did not like sailing, unlike his late wife, and that she being employed could not take the time off work anyway. It was O.K. for him because he was retired but un-like last Summer his friend could not come with him so he was on his own.

I am always amazed how much one finds out about people on the briefest of acquaintance!

Finally, I spied the "Iseult" the beautiful old Yawl that had been next to me on the pontoon in Guernsey, moored near the harbour entrance.

8

TRÉBEURDEN
TO L'ABERWRAC'H

Tuesday the 29ᵗʰ June, 2010.

0630 Woken by the yacht next to me leaving. Had a cup of tea and some Muisli and made out the Passage Plan from Trébeurden to L'AberWrac'h. Total distance 44 miles.

0755 Cast off from the pontoon in Trébeurden.

0810 Gourdec Abeam. Streamed log (Zeroed). Course 245 (T) Distance 3 miles to my turning point in the sea. Eng Revs 1400. Speed through the water 5.1 knots. Speed over the ground 3.9 knots. Wind Force 1 to 2 dead on the nose! Sea-state calm with a slight swell.

0840 Le Crapaud Buoy abeam to Starboard about 1 ½ miles away. Log 2.40. Altered course towards Le Pot de Fer East Cardinal Buoy. Course 265 (T). Distance 7 miles.

0910 Just passed a long line of small black birds sitting on the water. I thought until I got closer that they were the floats of a fishing net belonging to a white fishing vessel close by on my Starboard bow. Obviously I am interested because I do not want my propellers caught up in a net! I can also see one yacht motor-sailing with mainsail up who is overtaking me. She is about 1 ½ miles away on my Starboard Quarter.

0915 The white fishing boat is now abeam to Starboard about ¼ mile away. I can clearly see her crew working on deck through the binoculars.

0950 The "Plateau de la Méloine" is now abeam. I am now

in the channel known as "Toull-tan-Braz". Les Chaises de Primel are to Port. I can see what they mean. The row of rocks do look a bit like chairs sticking up out of the sea! Two yachts are passing me to Starboard coming the other way and a ketch going the other way also passes me to Port. The overtaking vessel already mentioned is now abeam to Starboard and there is another sailing vessel coming towards me from ahead. The latter turns out to be a "Feeling 326" and she passes to Port. I think they are also running their engine given that their jib keeps collapsing and yet they are making reasonable speed through the water.

1000 During the last hour we have made good 4.3 miles over the ground. The sky is covered with cloud and it looks like rain in the not too distant future. Wind SW Force 1-2. A French sailing yacht is crossing ahead under power. A woman is steering while a man is fishing off the stern. There are two very small fishing boats nearby---one of them is an inflatable! There are 3 people in the latter all fishing---1 girl and 2 boys.

1010 Another small fishing vessel crossing ahead. This time a small speedboat.

1015 I have just passed a very small sailing yacht to Starboard which cannot be more than 16 feet long and has one man in it also fishing! I can now see the houses in the town of Primel very closely to Port.

1025 Set Mainsail, Jib and Staysail.

1030 Log 11.49. A fishing boat passed close by to Port. There are a lot of pot markers around me. Just now I mistook two white birds for markers and altered course to avoid them! The Île de Batz can be seen fine on the Port bow in the distance.

Away over to Port is the former Episcopal city of St Pol de Léon. Its cathedral was begun in the 13th century on the site of an earlier church and completed in the 16th century. This place is also famous because of the battle which was fought here. This was a minor action during the Breton war of succession and thus part of the larger Hundred Years War.

It is important to remember the dominance of England in this part of the World at that time and the Battle of St Pol de Léon is an example of one of the many that were fought then. In 1346 the commander of the Anglo-Breton faction was Sir Thomas Dagworth a veteran professional soldier who had served under King Edward III of England for many years and was trusted to conduct the Breton war in an effective manner. Meanwhile Edward was raising money in England for his planned invasion of Normandy for the following year which eventually resulted in the crushing defeat of the French at the battle of Crécy.

Sir Thomas had problems. His forces were stretched across a handful of coastal towns and castles. His main opponent, Charles of Blois, was on the march with a substantial army of east Breton volunteers, French soldiers and German mercenaries.

To strengthen the resolve of his troops, Dagworth was conducting a tour of his domain along the North Coast of Brittany. This confirmed that he had support in the North and if the South fell he would have a line of retreat to England if the worst happened.

On the 9th June, 1346 Sir Thomas was in the Finistère region, moving North from the town of Morlaix, the scene of his earlier victory in the Battle of Morlaix.

Blois then led the fastest elements of his army North in a surprise attack and ambushed Dagworth and his 180 man bodyguard at the isolated village of Saint-Pol-de-Léon.

Dagworth responded by forming up his men and leading them in a rapid withdrawal towards a nearby hill, where they dug trenches and prepared positions.

Blois was an intelligent general and he had already seen and noted the ruthless efficiency of the English longbow at Morlaix and in numerous other smaller skirmishes. He knew that cavalry would be doomed on the slopes of the hill and that the only way to break the English position and capture Dagworth before relief could arrive was a direct frontal assault with infantry.

To this end he dismounted all his soldiers and abandoned his horse himself and ordered his superior number of troops to make a three pronged attack on the Anglo-Breton lines. This assault and all the others that afternoon were repulsed by accurate archery fire. There was also some last ditch hand to hand fighting.

The final assault came at last light with Charles himself in the vanguard, but even this failed to achieve victory and the Franco-Breton forces were forced to abandon their attack and return to eastern Brittany leaving behind dozens of their dead, wounded and captured soldiers on the hillside.

The Anglo-Breton forces had suffered lightly and despite a number of serious injuries, none of the knights or men-at-arms had been killed while losses amongst the archers and the rank and file were low. The real effect of the battle was psychological. Charles of Blois, who had a reputation as a fierce and intelligent commander had been defeated by an English commander and one of common stock at that. Indeed, Charles failed to win a single one of the five significant battles he fought against the English between 1342 and 1364. The Breton nobility had now been given food for thought in choosing which side to back in the on-going war!

1050 There is a small fishing vessel crossing close ahead. We are now passing Roscoff where the ferry from Cork comes in. Roscoff used to be a port for pirates!

1110 Furled jib as the wind has swung round right on the nose. Speed through the water 4.5 knots. Revs 1250. Mainsail and staysail hard in but shaking.

1118 Log 14.99. Aston East Cardinal Buoy abeam to Port. Distance about 1/3 of a mile. Increased engine revs to 1400. Speed through the water 4.7 knots. Wind dead on our nose Force 1 to 2.

1125 Suddenly the seas are heaping up in great lumps. I altered course to Starboard 10 degrees to avoid the breaking seas straight ahead. I imagine that this is turbulence caused by an uneven bottom. Speed through the water 4.2 knots---it has been reduced because Tarla is being thrown around so much. Wind F2 from straight ahead.

1130 Log 15.71. The lighthouse on the Île de Batz is now abeam to Port. We are now climbing 2 metre lumps of water and the speed through the water is 4.3 knots. The waves are breaking close on the Port beam. Speed over the ground 7.0 knots. Altered Course to 309 (T) to avoid being swept into the breaking waves. Tarla is now putting both noses under the sea at times and rearing up like a young colt. I had to take over the steering as the autopilot couldn't cope and speed at times was down to 2 knots through the water as the propellers came close to the surface but to be fair they never raced.

1200 Altered course to 255 (T) for Aman ar Ross North Cardinal Buoy. Distance 18 miles. Log 17.69. Speed through the water 4.0 knots. Speed over the ground 6.0 knots. A German yacht crossed my bows from Starboard to Port. I now realise that I have just come through a tidal race off the Île de Batz. There is no mention of this race on the chart nor in the pilot book that I have. But it is my own silly fault. I am old enough to know that you treat headlands with respect especially in waters such as these coming up to spring tides. Luckily there was not much wind as it would be fearsome with wind against tide. What I should have done was to give the headland a much wider berth and not try to cut the corner. Two or three miles offshore would have been fine.

Most visitors to the Île de Batz (pronounced 'ba') make a beeline for the "Jardin Exotique Georges Delaselle" in the South-East of the island. This extraordinary garden was created between 1897 and 1937 by a Parisian businessman. The garden has more than 2,000 species of plant in it from all five continents. It boasts a superb collection of palm trees. None of these species would grow, of course, without the temperate climate caused by the Gulf Stream. Georges Delaselle also unearthed a Bronze Age burial site within his grounds.

The island's sailors had as their patron St. Anne and they prayed to her in the 11th century "Chapelle Ste Anne". The dedication of this book and the meaning of this coincidence are not lost on me after what I have just come through!

At the wild Western end of Batz is the 'Trou du Serpent' (Snake's Hole). The name refers to the place where, according to legend, St. Pol cast a dragon which was terrorising the island. Of Irish interest is that one of the island's main activities is collecting seaweed which is sold to pharmaceutical, food processing and cosmetic companies.

The lighthouse on the Île de Batz was built in the 19th century and is 45 metres high and 75 metres above sea-level. There are 198 steps to the top!

1230 I celebrated leaving the Île de Batz behind by eating the last slice of Anne's cake and having a cup of tea.

1300 I have just calculated that we have done 24 miles over the ground since we started. We still have 11 miles to go to Aman ar Ross Buoy and a further 8 miles to the Libenter Buoy which marks the outside limit of the channel into L'AberWrac'h.

1315 Out here on the sea the land is a hazy strip. It is sunny with a thin layer of cloud spread over the sky. We are coming up to a headland called Pointe de Beg Pol.

1400 Log 25.50. Revs 1400. Speed through the water 4.0 knots. Speed over the ground 5.5 knots. Wind WNW Force 3. [Stronger than it was]. Course 260 (T). The sails are stalled as the wind is very fine on the Starboard bow. We have made good 6.2 miles in the last hour. From the chart-plotter we have 5 miles to go to Aman ar Ross Buoy. Tarla is starting to slam and hobbyhorse now as the head wind builds up the sea. Another yacht flying a big balloon spinnaker is coming the other way closer inshore.

1430 The sea is building. Wind over tide. [About 1 ½ metres high]. Tarla is "slamming" with "thumps" from under the bridgedeck.

1450 increased revs to 1500.

1500 Log 29.23. Revs 1500. Speed through the water 4.5 knots. Speed over the ground 5.2. Course 253 (T). Aman ar Ross North Cardinal Buoy abeam to Port.

1515 A yacht to Port of me is trying to make Lizen von Quest Buoy like me. A small white motor boat (fishing) is crossing my bow.

Île Verge Lighthouse looks stupendous as it should. It is one of the tallest lighthouses in the World. You have to climb 365 steps to reach the top! It was in the 19th century that engineers really got to grips with the great challenge of making Brittany's fearsome coasts safer by building a string of vast lighthouses with powerful beams. The Phare de l'Île Vierge was built relatively late, at the start of the 20th century. Nevertheless, it was a tremendous technical feat as it is over 80 metres high and can be seen far along the coast in each direction. The beam from the light can be seen from more than 50 kilometres away on a clear night. This makes it one of the most powerful lighthouses in the world although it is second to Le Creac'h on Ouessant. One of the islands near Île Vierge was used by the Americans to build a base for their seaplanes in the First World War although it never became operational.

1620 Increased revs to 1600. Speed through the water 4.4 kns. Speed over the ground 3.2 knots. The tide has turned!

1700 The Libenter Buoy is in sight! Log 38.11. Speed through the water 5.0. Speed over the ground 2.5 knots. Course 229 (T). I then altered course to 210 (T). A yacht under sail passed me to Starboard going the other way.

I've just noticed that they have windmills ashore which they didn't have when I arrived in "Chang O" seven years ago. [The "Chang O" was a Junk Rigged Kingfisher 20+ with an outboard motor in which I cruised single-handed from Cork to Southern Brittany and back in 2003]. I am now overtaking a small sailing sloop on my starboard side which has a red hull and a cream deck which I think is actually sailing. There is another yacht further out which is motoring the other way.

1740 Libenter Buoy abeam close on my Port side so hauled log reading 41.62. Set course for red buoy which marks the channel in and I can see "Le pot de petit Beurre" marker in the distance. Set revs at 1000 under Mainsail and Staysail. Speed through the water 4.8 knots. Speed over the ground 5.4 knots.

1758 'Petit pot de Beurre' abeam to Port. Set the jib. Wind on the beam.

1800 Stopped the engine just to have the peace of sailing for a little while after the noise of the diesel all day. SUCH SILENCE! We are sailing at 3.3 knots through the water while I rig the fenders and mooring lines on both sides with the autopilot doing the steering.

1845 Tied up to the wave-breaker in L'AberWrac'h Marina. A man came to collect the money which came to E20-60 with no surcharge for catamarans. Tidied up and went and looked at the "Meteo" pinned up outside the Capitannerie. The wind tomorrow is forecast to be SSW Force 3 or 4. On my nose for Cameret so I wont be going!

1900 Cooked myself something to eat and washed it down with ½ bottle of red wine.

1930 Started the trek for fuel. Put 30 litres into the tank which I am now beginning to think must hold 80 litres! It must do because it was more than half full before I started.

2100 My friend Peter Spry-Leverton rang. He proposes to sail from Cameret to L'AberWrac'h in his Peter Duck Ketch tomorrow as the wind is fair. This suits me! I don't want another day of motoring into a head wind.

I have now passed the 400 mile mark since leaving Walton-on-Naze. I am also in the place where I landed from "Chang O" seven years ago having completed the overnight voyage from the Scilly Islands. Life is good. If only Anne was here.

9

L'ABERWRAC'H
TO CAMERET.

Tuesday the 29th of June, 2010.

The man and woman in the motor cruiser ahead of me on the pontoon are both from County Kerry in Ireland although their boat is flying the "Red Duster". They are returning from Turkey having spent the last 8 years living there. They are waiting for good weather before crossing to Newlyn and thence to Cork. Opposite me across the "wave-breaker" is a huge motor yacht (Must be 70 or 80 feet long) with a British gentleman as owner. The Irish boat is about 40 feet by 14 feet.

2300 Turned in.

Wednesday the 30th of June, 2010.

0730 Got up and went round the harbour taking photos.

Tom Cunliffe in "The Shell Channel Pilot" has this to say about L'AberWrach.

"L'AberWrac'h is famous for its strategic importance, good shelter and ready accessibility in all but strong North Westerly gales. Facilities have greatly improved with the building of the new Marina although one still has to walk two miles to get to a shop! It makes an ideal place to gather one's wits for the Chanel de Four. Upriver, a pleasant soujourn can be passed in peace and tranquillity,"

Indeed, on my previous trip on the "Chang O" seven years ago I did spend a very pleasant "soujourn" here up the river rafted up with Peter and Joe on the "Anadina" and Mike and Sally in their Vancouver 34 [pilothouse version]. It became, as the sun set, almost like a page out of "Swallows and Amazons" by Arthur Ransome. That occasion will live long in my memory.

One theory is that l'Aberwrac'h derives its name from the first immersed rock of its channel which is called "Ar Grach" which means "The Old Woman". An alternative theory is that the name is derived from the "Estuary of the Fairy" which may be related to the alleged Gallo-Roman bridge located upstream of the river mouth and called "The Bridge of the Devil" who's ruins can still be seen today.

0830 Had a cup of tea and some Muesli.

Had another conversation with the two motor boat owners above. The Irish boat the "Castlevar" is 43 feet long and cruises at 6 knots with a maximum speed of 8 knots. There is only one engine but huge fuel tanks. They fill up where fuel is cheapest and the last time was in Gibraltar before making their way up the Portuguese coast and crossing the Bay of Biscay. The big motor yacht the "Orinoco" is based in Falmouth and has cruised with just the man and his wife as far as Dingle, the West coast of Scotland and down to Southern Brittany. Although the maximum speed with their twin diesels is 23 knots it is quite uneconomic. They use 45 litres of diesel (ph) at 9 knots and 60 litres of diesel (ph) at 10 knots so they tend to stick to the former. They made the passage across from Falmouth to L'Aber Wrach in under 12 hours burning less than 500 litres of diesel! Interestingly, her owner said that she cost only 5% of her capital cost to run and this included depreciation on the capital sum invested!

0900---1200 Did some more typing concerning the "Tarla's" voyage.

1200---1400 Cleaned ship and tidied up.

1400 Had a beer and then went and paid 2 nights harbour dues [E20---60 per night with no surcharge for cats]. Then walked the 2 miles to Landeda where the nearest supermarket is situated.

1600 Had a very late lunch.

1900 Peter phoned to say that he and the "Anadina" were off "Le petit Beure".

1930 The "Anadina" tied up to a pontoon.

2000 Went with Peter to a restaurant and had a meal. We both came back to the "Tarla" afterwards and drank whiskey.

2400 Turned in.

Thursday the 1st of July.

0700 Got up! Had usual cup of tea and Muesli. I appear to be getting a radio signal on the computer. Will have to contact Niall later when he has woken up.

1100 Had coffee with Peter on board the "Tarla" and eat the first of Judith Harrington's cake which she had so kindly given me in Eastbourne. Like Anne's cake it was excellent. Whilst we were having coffee the "Orinoco" sailed.

1300 Walked with Peter to Landeda and had a very pleasant cup of coffee in the village "Tabac" as the supermarket [where I came yesterday] was closed until 1500 for lunch!

1600 Talked to Niall on the phone. Managed to connect to WIFI Brest. Answered e-mails. Surfed the web for information concerning the weather.

1800 Went aboard the "Anadina" for pre-dinner drinks and then dined in a local restaurant.

2200 Returned aboard the "Tarla" for a "nightcap" which consisted of two glasses of whiskey each.

2400 Turned in.

Friday the 2nd of July, 2010.

0700 Got up and went back to bed again as it was pouring with rain.

0900 Got up---still pouring with rain!

0940 Went to the post office to buy stamps and send off postcards.

10000 Did the washing up and made out my passage plan for tomorrow.

1100 Peter arrived for morning coffee and some of Judith's cake. The weather forecast is looking good tomorrow for both Peter and myself. Peter is crossing the English Channel to Fowey in Cornwall and I will be going to Cameret through the Chanel de Four.

1500 Still raining! Peter and I had cups of tea on the "Tarla" until it stopped and then filled the "Anadina" up with diesel for her coming trip. I also purchased an extra 10 litres of diesel for myself.

1700 Went for drinks in the yacht club followed by dinner in a restaurant. Came back to the "Tarla" for whiskey. Had two phone calls from Anne. Checked out the weather for Peter on the internet and went to bed.

Saturday the 3rd of July.

0500 Got up and waved goodbye to the Irish couple who left at first light at 0600 bound for Newlyn in Cornwall in the "Castlevar". All being well they should make it before it gets dark. They were nice people. I listened to the shipping forecast and prepared the "Tarla" for the coming voyage.

0700---0930 Went back to bed.

1000 Had a cup of tea with Peter on the "Tarla".

1040 Started engine and let it warm up while I waited for Peter to cast off. I have all my instruments on and the wind is NNE Force 1 to 2.

1050 I cast off from the pontoon and proceeded to sea under engine following the "Anadina". On the way I hoisted my mainsail which did its usual trick of jamming. On the way out to the Lebenter Buoy I have never seen it so rough (in the 12 or so visits that I have made to this port) as the great Atlantic swells came rolling in. On a number of occasions the "Tarla" put her twin noses right under and unfortunately I had left the cabin hatch slightly open and the lumps of solid water crashing on to it sent water below soaking the cabin floor.

1110 Lebenter Buoy abeam. I waved goodbye to Peter which bought back memories of doing the same thing 7 years ago when I was sailing the "Chang O" to Penzance and Peter was sailing the "Anadina" to Fowey. The difference between the two occasions, apart from the fact that I was in a different boat, was that today the sea was much rougher and seven years ago thick fog had suddenly rolled in so that we lost sight of each other very quickly.

1112 Streamed Log (zeroed). Course 250 (T). Distance to "Basse Pampian" East Cardinal Buoy 6 miles. Speed through the water 5.3 knots. Speed over the ground 4.9. Engine revs 1400. Very lumpy 2 metre swell.

1200 Just caught thick weed round both propellers which stalled the engine. I really did not like the thought of having to climb overboard to cut it free when the "Tarla" was being thrown around so much by the swell! So I started the engine again with the hydraulic motor valves in neutral. Then by taking one side at a time and by putting the motor ahead and then immediately astern and then ahead again and so on I managed to shake the weed free. I then followed out the same process on the other side. Underway again I found that speed through the water was 5.1 knots at 1400 revs so I must have cleared the weed away fully and no damage was done. The log read 1.53.

1236 Grand Bass de Portsall east Cardinal Buoy abeam to Starboard. Log 4.32. Speed through the water 5.0 knots. Speed over the ground 5.6 knots.

1247 "Basse Pampion" East Cardinal Buoy abeam to Port. Log 5.0. Altered course for a position one mile off Le Four Lighthouse. Course 210(T). Distance 4 miles.

1300 Log 6.03. Speed through the water 5.3 knots. Speed

over the ground 5.0 knots. Course 210(T). Plotted position on the chart and discovered that the "Tarla" has made good 5 miles in the last hour.

1315 I tried 3 times to communicate with Peter by VHF radio on channel 8 as we had previously arranged but to no avail. This means that either he has forgotten and has his set switched off, or that he cannot hear it because of the noise of his engine or, me being pessimistic by nature, my new VHF set can only receive but not transmit! From the top of my mast to the top of his there should be a direct line between our two aerials as we cannot be more than 20 miles apart.

1320 I can see through the binoculars the big swells breaking on Le Four lighthouse. It makes a most spectacular sight.

1330 Le Four lighthouse abeam. Log 8.59. Altered course to 180(T) for La Valbelle Buoy. Distance 5 miles. Speed through the water 5.4 knots. Speed over the ground 5.5. The mainsail is now filling (Just!).

1340 Reduced to 1200 revs. Speed through the water 4.7 knots. Speed over the ground 4.8. The "Tarla" has just overtaken a French motor-sailor with a green hull close to Port and a bit further away to Port I am keeping pace with a German ketch. Despite my very best efforts to avoid it I have just run over some more weed that got caught round the propellers. This time the engine did not stall and after a few moments picked up again. Thank God!

1400 Log 11.22. Course 180(T). Speed through the water 4.7 knots. Speed over the ground 4.6 knots. Set staysail. Ushant is now abeam to Starboard. I am clearly in the Chanel de Four!

The island of Ushant (Ouessant in French) is 18 miles off the Breton coast of Le Conquet. The Pointe de Pem is France's most Westerly point. One of the rocks there is painted white to act as a marker for seamen. On the tip of the point is a ruin, known as the "Villa des Tempêtes", which housed a steam foghorn from 1885 to 1900.

More than 50,000 ships a year round Ushant as they enter or leave the English Channel and as a result there are six lighthouses around the island. The best known is "Creac'h", which has one of the most powerful lights in the World. Its beam can be seen more than 80 kilometres away on a clear night. The lighthouse to the East of the island is known as "Le Stiff" and is another prominent landmark. It was designed by the engineer Vauban in 1695.

There are many wrecks around Ushant. One of the more famous was the "Drummond Castle" which went ashore in 1896 while returning from South Africa to England. All on board perished. Another more recent wreck was the tanker the "Amoco Cadiz" which went ashore in 1978 causing a huge oil spill which polluted the Breton coast.

Lampaul is the island's main village with about 900 inhabitants and its cemetery is full of unknown sailors and lists of ships that are no more. Small wax crosses represent someone lost at sea and this is known as the Proella tradition.

As well as welcoming around 400 species of bird Ushant's most famous residents are the 600 small black faced sheep. These sheep represent one of the smallest breeds known to man.

1410 La Valbelle Buoy is in sight. The chart-plotter says 2.6 miles away and the swell has gone down a lot due to the protection of Ushant to Starboard. The sea is now glasslike and the two sails are just about filled by the wind. It has turned out to be a nice day with a whole group of yachts going through ahead of me and my two companion yachts where I am slightly in the lead coming with me. There are 15 windmills on the mainland shore which weren't there 7 years ago.

1443 La Valbelle Buoy Abeam to Port. Log 14.32. Altered course to 170(T) for Rouget Buoy. Distance 4.5 miles.

1535 Rouget Abeam to Starboard. Log 12.22.

1615 Pointe de St. Mathieu Abeam together with Les Vieux Moines (both in transit). Log 21.55. Altered course to 105(T).

Large merchant ship coming out of the Rade de Brest up ahead and there is also a yacht sailing in the same direction as myself half a mile away on my Starboard beam.

I have just been passed by 6 yachts going the other way to catch the flood tide through the Chanel de Four. The last of the 6 is a yacht called "Mr. Robinson" and he is flying a huge German Ensign !

1625 There is a merchant ship loaded with containers passing ahead of me about 2 miles away. The scenery is absolutely stupendous with the light making different patterns on the rocks which stick out of the sea like teeth.

1700 Log 25.80. Speed through the water 5.7 knots. Speed over the ground 5.5 knots. Mainsail eased off as the wind is now over the quarter Force 2/3. I can now see right into the Rade de Brest and there are an awful lot of sailing yachts inside. In my immediate vicinity there are at least 20 yachts all sailing either coming or going from Cameret or the Rade de Brest.

A handful of very well protected peninsulas stretch out inside the Rade de Brest which forms a huge landlocked bay. In the past religious men founded abbeys in these privileged locations, such as that at Daoulas. The abbey at Daoulas, like that of nearby Landevernec, has its origins going back to the dark ages, but the buildings that you see today date from medieval times. They include a rare Romanesque cloister, alongside which a medieval medicinal herb garden has been recreated. Nearer Brest, Plougastel-Daoulas is reputed in France both for its Calvary and its delicious strawberries. Unfortunately, it suffered from heavy bombing raids during the Second World War. Its famous 17th century calvary was badly damaged, but thanks to an American officer, John. D. Skilton, who became passionate about the place's history, the Calvary was lovingly restored. The 180 figures sport fine costumes. They were all carved out of the distinctive Kersanton stone which was quarried nearby. Carvings made from this stone are to be found all over Brittany.

1743 Pointe du Grande Gouin Abeam to Starboard. Log 29.41 [Handed log]. Dropped mainsail. Furled staysail. Put fenders and mooring lines out on both sides.

There have been problems with the self steering over the last 6 miles. The "Tarla" keeps wandering off her course and you have to keep bringing her back and re-setting the autopilot. There is a lot of problem with constantly having to avoid the thick clumps of weed in the water which could potentially foul the propellers and in addition the fishermen's buoys, of which there seem to be a lot around here, are a constant hazard.

1830 Tied up to a pontoon in the inner harbour in Cameret. Paid E52-50 for 2 nights berthing [There is a 50% surcharge for cats, the first time that this has happened since leaving Walton]. It is very crowded. Three of us are rafted up with the "Tarla" in the middle. The French yacht outside of me is housing at least 6 people plus a Pekinese dog that has to be taken ashore frequently! The yacht is a Bavaria 36. There is a mother and father, 3 teenage girls and another man.

1930 Cooked beans, sausages and peas. Eat cake and a banana and washed the whole lot down with 2 glasses of red wine. Read my book and relaxed after sending my usual texts.

2230 Turned in.

10

CAMERET
TO THE ÎLES DE GLÉNAN

Sunday 4th July, 2010.

0730 Got up and had a cup of tea. Looked at the Pilot concerning the Raz de Sein. It had the following to say:

"The Raz de Sein can be rough, especially in the overfalls off La Vielle, even in moderate winds if they are contrary to the stream. When wind and tide are together the passage is smoother than outside. In light weather, at neap tides and in the absence of swell, the passage can be made at any time under power, but the seas caused by the irregular bottom knock the way off a boat very quickly. Except when wind and tide are together, slack water for the passage is always to be preferred. The Raz is temperamental and the seas met there vary considerably, but in strong winds contrary to the stream the overfalls are dangerous. There is a fair weather anchorage in which to wait for the tide in the Baie des Trépassés---the Bay of Corpses---so called as it is here that bodies of those shipwrecked on the Raz often come ashore."

"Slack water as the north going flood expires, occurs between about Brest minus 1 and Brest minus ½. If Southbound aim for the middle of that window plus or minus 15 minutes."

High Water Brest tomorrow, Monday, is at 1132 French Summer Time. So "Window" is between 1032 and 1102. Say it takes 4 hours to get there I would have to leave Cameret at about 0645.

0815 Received a text from Peter saying that he had arrived safely in Polruan [opposite Fowey] in the "Anadina" after a 21 hour passage. Not bad for 105 miles.

0830---1030 Did some more typing of the log on my computer.

1030 Went Shopping.

1200 Had Lunch. Baguette, Pâté, Cheese and a pint of Beer.

1230---1700 Did further typing concerning the voyage.

1250 The Motor Cruiser leaving ahead was blown sideways onto my bows. No damage done as I managed to fend him off.

1400 Both my inside and outside neighbours decided to leave. The skipper of the Bavaria 36 on the outside turned out to be a recently retired Captain of a French Ferry sailing between Dover and Calais. He had spent 33 years at sea. [He is probably only about 50 years old]. Both my neighbours had difficulty getting out because of the onshore breeze and I was extremely grateful for my twin props as I "jilled around" waiting for the inside boat to depart. After their departure I came in alongside the pontoon and moored up. Having just tied up again an old man asked me in French whether the flag on the stern of the "Tarla" was Swedish because he had not seen it before! He was delighted, as was his friend, when I told him that it was Irish!

1700 Stopped typing as I had had enough! Put the computer away and poured myself a glass of red wine. [I have done 6 ½ hours of typing today].

The weather looks like rain tomorrow morning with visibility reduced to 3 miles. I think I will stay here another day and let the weather front go through. It looks as if it is going to be nice on Tuesday and even better on Wednesday and Thursday. All I need is four clear days to get to Étel !

1800 Finished Michael Harrington's book which I must say is excellent and I strongly recommend it to others [It concerns "Lane's Story" and was presented to me by him in Eastbourne]. He made a good job of it.

2200 Turned in.

Monday the 5th of July, 2010.

0800 Got up to find a blue sky and strong sunshine! There had obviously been heavy rain during the night but it had passed over. Such is timing! I could have gone this morning but now it is too late. The "Meteo" said "Morning" for the restricted visibility and the rain. However, I expect the weather to improve in the next few days based on my detailed perusal of the synoptic chart. One cannot take risks with the Raz. Had a cup of tea. There are still a lot of dark clouds around. It may rain yet!

0815 Raining!

0830---1030 Did some more typing!

1030 The weather looks as if it is clearing up. Although it is still cloudy the black ones have gone. Went shopping. Paid the man in the Capitanerie E26-50 for another nights stay [50% surcharge for catamarans].

1130---1230 Worked out the passage plan for tomorrow. Put briefly I have to be at the Raz between 1138 and 1208 and estimating my average speed as 5 knots I should therefore start from Cameret at 0738 which means 0700! The current between Cameret and La Vielle Lighthouse will be against us but is not strong in the Douarnenez bay which we will be crossing. Having rounded the Raz the tide turns in our favour at High Water Brest which is at 1238. It will then run in our favour for 4 hours.

As usual, as in all my passage plans I then worked out the courses to steer and the distances between all the important landmarks, buoys etc that I would encounter as well as alternative plans if anything went wrong along the way.

1245 Had lunch---Beer, Baguette, Cheese, Pâté and Apple.

There are two identical Westerly Fulmars astern of me. They came in last night and moored side by side. On the one called "Fearless" registered in Southampton there is a single man and on the other called "Aswas", registered in Falmouth, are two men and a woman. The average age of all four is definitely 60+!

1315 I have just checked the engine oil. It is dirty but so far

I don't seem to have used any.

1330 Continued to work on typing up the log.

1700 Finished typing and did the washing up.

1730 Poured myself a glass of red wine and read my book in the cockpit. It is a very pleasant sunny evening with a light breeze. The weather forecast for tomorrow is for a wind of SW Force 2 with a visibility of 2 to 5 miles in the morning and SW Force 3 with a visibility of 10 miles in the afternoon.

1900 Made myself a salad and had some of Judith's cake for pudding. Limited myself to half a bottle of wine.

2000 Went for a walk and visited the sailor's chapel which is dedicated to Our lady [Notre Dame]. I took photos of it from outside and then more photos of Vauban's Fort which is close by.

Cameret-sur-Mer is a town built along the edge of the harbour and because of its strategic position has figured in many wars. The old fort on Le Sillon, on the North side of the harbour, and La Tour Doree near the Marina which I have just photographed were designed by Vauban and date from 1689. Five years after their construction the defences repelled a combined Dutch and English attack and in 1791 they won a victory against 5 English Frigates. In "Eyes of the Admiralty J.T. Serres : An Artist in the Channel Fleet 1799---1800" by M.K. Barritt the "Anse de Cameret" is clearly depicted as are the rocks off "Pointe St. Mathieu" which are known as "Les Vieux Moines" and there is a very fine picture of "Le Goulet" which is the entrance to the "Rade de Brest".

Camaret used to be a very active fishing port specialising in tuna fish and lobster. Camaret fishing boats would leave for months on end to fish along the shores of distant coasts. This explains the origins of the bawdy song "The Girls of Camaret" as their men-folk were missing and for so long.

Camaret is a great "crossroads" for yachts bound North or South across the Bay of Biscay. For example, at 4 knots average speed, it takes 80 hours to reach La Coruna in Spain.

2100 Had a whiskey and did the washing up.

2200 Set the alarm for 0600 and turned in.

Tuesday the 6th of July, 2010.

0600 Got up and had the usual cup of tea. Rigged all the instruments. Singled up etc.

0650 Left the pontoon in Cameret inner harbour. Passed the "Crabber" the "Belle Étoile" on the way out. She was moored alongside the pontoon in the outer harbour.

"La Belle Étoile" was built to the plans of a previous vessel of the same name. The original was constructed in 1938 at the Chantier Naval Gourmelon de Camaret-sur-Mer for Auguste Kergroac'h. The new version, also built in Camaret in Le Chantier Naval d'Albert Péron in 1992, sails to various festivals of the sea and takes out paying passengers for day trips and short cruises. She is 26.25 metres long overall. The length of hull is 18 metres. Her beam is 5.7 metres. Her draft 3 metres. Her sail area 252 square metres with six sails. She has three crew and can carry nine passengers. Her tonnage is 33.

0700 Hoisted mainsail. Increased revs to 1200. Speed through the water 4.5 knots. Speed over the ground 4.4 knots. There appear to be a considerable number of yachts making for the Raz ahead of me. It is a calm sunny morning with good visibility. Little Wind.

0710 Pointe Du Grande Goin Abeam. Streamed log (zeroed).

The entrance to the Rade de Brest which is now on my Starboard beam looks just as it did in Serres paintings in 1799.

0730 The Lighthouse on the Pointe de Toulinquet is abeam. Log 1.26.

0737 Turned into the Chanel du Toulinquet. This passage between the Pointe de Toulinquet and the off lying rocks, known as Le Pohen, is only a ¼ mile wide.

0742 Black and Yellow marker abeam to Port although you hug the Starboard side of the channel going this way through.

Log 2.15. Just passed Le Louveteau which is a shallow spot in the middle which we have left to Port.

About a mile ahead are big lumps of rocks at least 100 feet high sticking out of the sea. It looks as if we are sailing straight at them.

0745 We are now passing less than one cable from the rocks on Le Pohen. There is a rock at the end of Le Pohen known as Le Lion and it looks just like one! There is also a huge rock with a big hole in it which I am now looking straight through.

0750 Altered course for La Vielle Lighthouse 200(T). Distance 15 miles. Le Lion abeam. Log 2.82. Engine revs 1200. Speed through the water 4.8 knots. Speed over the ground 4.4. I have just been overtaken on the Port side by a yacht under mainsail motor-sailing. She is flying the British flag.

0800 There is a big Buoy to Starboard not marked on my chart and the seas are breaking around it---maybe a large wreck. I am now abeam of it. Log 3.56. Speed through the water 4.8 knots. Speed over the ground 4.0 knots. Course 200(T).

0808 Le Tas de Pois Ouest Abeam to Port. Log 4.09. Course 200(T). We are now clear of the rocks in the Chanel du Toulinquet so I made a cup of tea and eat some cake! Pointe du Van is clearly in view on the horizon although it is more than 10 miles away. The bay of Douarnenez is opening up to Port. I am following the yacht which overtook me which is now broad on my Port bow. The considerable number of yachts which I thought were going to the Raz earlier have now all vanished. Most of them altered course and went into the Rade de Brest before I turned into the Chanel du Toulinquet. There is a big tanker passing astern of me off my Starboard quarter going into Brest and there is another yacht far out at sea motor-sailing with her mainsail set for the Raz [Probably came through the Chanel de Four].

0830 There is a yacht crossing my bow in the distance going into the bay of Douarnenez. She is attempting to sail in what is a very light wind of about Force 1 from a direction of which I am not quite sure. There is a slight swell which rocks us gently.

0845 Cap de la Chèvre Abeam to Port. Log 7.00. One yacht with no sail set can be seen off the end of it.

Le Cap de la Chèvre is at the Southern end of the Crozon peninsular and Camaret-sur-Mer is at the Northern end. Hidden from me behind the peninsular is the fishing port of Morgat. The latter has the remains of an 18th century gun battery and a 19th century barracks. Also hidden is the even smaller port of Rostudal. During the first weekend of August each year there is a World music festival in the town of Crozon known as the "Festival du Bout du Monde". Here enthusiasts can hear the sounds of Glastonbury re-enacted! Crozon is also home to the French fleet of nuclear submarines. There are many flora and fauna on this peninsular but the most unique is the small blue flower known as "crozonnaise". The tower on the tip of Cap de la Chèvre is a lookout post for the French Navy.

0900 Log 8.06. Course 200(T). Speed through the water 4.8 knots. Speed over the ground 4.4. I plotted the "Tarla's" position on the chart and we have 9.5 miles to La Vielle Lighthouse still to go. The yacht that could be seen off Cap de la Chèvre is obviously heading for the Chanel du Toulinquet. La Vielle lighthouse is now in sight ahead.

0925 The bay of Douarnanez is now completely open. I thought of Richard and Hilary sailing their big Essex smack "Salley" without an engine all the way from Maldon in Essex to the first big meeting of traditional boats in Douarnanez and Brest in the early 1990's. To me this seems to be an extraordinary achievement.

Douarnenez lies at the mouth of the Pouldavid Estuary on the Southern shore of Douarnenez Bay. The legendary city of "Ys", of Breton folklore, is believed to lie below the bay. The port is also associated with the medieval story of Tristan, lover of Iseult, for whom Tristan Island is named.

The written history of Douarnenez begins around 1118

when according to a charter dated 1126, Robert de Locuvan, Bishop of Cornouáille, donated the island of St. Tutuarn [In the 14th century re-named St Tristan] and the lands belonging to it to the Abbey of Marmoutier.

The fishing history of Douarnenez goes back to Gallo-Roman times when, as archeological finds demonstrate, fish were salted along the cliffs of Plomarc'h. In the years before the French Revolution, sardines became the driving force for the local economy, culminating in huge fishing and canning activities at the beginning of the 20th century. The strikes in the 1920's in favour of better working conditions for the factory women known as "Penn Sardin" were the main reason why Douarnenez became one of the first communist municipalities in France.

Since 1986 Douarnenez has organised maritime festivals once every two years bringing together all types of traditional sailing vessel, with competitors from the four corners of the earth. In 2004, a record year, there were almost 2000 sailing vessels, 17,000 sailors and 30 participating countries.

There are a lot of windmills on the tops of the cliffs leading in from Pointe Van towards Douarnanez. They weren't there 7 years ago! I am still keeping station with the yacht motor sailing off my Port bow. She is about ¼ of a mile away.

0945 The yacht ahead on the port bow has reduced speed. I am now overhauling her so I reduce my engine revs to 1000. Speed through the water 4.2 knots. Speed over the ground 3.8. Log 11.70 Course 200(T). We have both realised that we are early! We need to reach La Vielle and La Plate off the Raz at 1153 plus or minus 15 minutes. A yacht has just come through the other way.

1000 The yacht above turns out to be Swedish and has just passed me to Port.[I altered course to Starboard to avoid her]. Log 12.60. Revs 1000. Speed through the water 4.2 knots. Speed over the ground 3.7. Course 200(T). 5 miles to go to La Vielle Lighthouse. The Plateau de Terenez with its very distinctive white Lighthouse is clearly in sight off the Starboard bow. In the distance is Le Chaussee de Sein or as the British in the time of Nelson would have called them "The Saints". The Île de Sein in the middle of the Chaussee can also be clearly seen. Four yachts are now coming up astern of me. Judging from their course I think that they all probably went through the Chanel de Four before crossing Douarnanez Bay. Another yacht, which is motoring, is crossing ahead of me coming from the Île de Sein.

Five miles off the Pointe du Raz, the Île de Sein is arguably Brittany's most unusual island, not least because it is entirely flat. The highest point is just 6 metres. The saying goes "qui voit Sein, voit sa fin" (he who sees Sein, sees his end) primarily because of the dangerous reefs in the area which have caused many shipwrecks. In fact the first inhabitants were castaways. The island is about two kilometres long by less than one kilometre wide. The only way to get around it is on foot. General de Gaule unveiled the Croix de Lorraine in 1960 as a tribute to the 140 male islanders of the Free French Movement that followed him into exile in England in World War Two. In the far West of the island is the Grand Phare which not only warns ships with its light but also is responsible for purifying the seawater and generating the electricity for the island homes.

As you would expect Sein is steeped in legend. The most famous is that of the nine virgins, a group of women who lived apart from the village and who were known for their healing powers and their ability to control the weather. During the Nepoleonic wars the British Navy often visited "The Saints" to press-gang the men. They were very highly regarded as seamen.

1030 Have had to alter course 20 degrees to Starboard in order to maintain our true course over the ground towards la Vielle. The current is setting us sideways towards the rocks on the mainland. Log 14.46. Speed through the water 4.0 knots. Speed over the ground 2.9 knots. Revs 1000. I plotted the Tarla's position on the chart and discovered that we have 3.5 miles to go to La Vielle. There is a big motor-yacht overtaking me and a small fishing boat and a yacht coming the other way. All will pass to Starboard of me.

The motor-yacht overtaking me is the "Orinoco" which was with me in L'AberWrach. She is flying the Blue Ensign. I wave enthusiastically but she turns out not to be the "Orinoco", although she is identical, as when she has passed I can see her stern through the binoculars. Her name begins with a 'P' but I am moving up and down too much to be able to focus the binoculars properly.

1045 I am being overtaken by a sailing yacht with just her mainsail set. The Île de Sein, which is very low lying is now very clearly in view on the Starboard bow and you can see that there are lots of houses on it. It appears to be built up almost from one end to the other.

1100 Pointe du Van abeam. The Baie des Trépassérs is opening up to Port. Log 16.40. Speed through the water 4.0 knots. Speed over the ground 3.3 knots. 2 miles to go to La Vielle. Course now 217(T) to clear La Plate. There is a motor fishing vessel crossing ahead of me at speed. I notice that my British friend in the yacht ahead is taking the inshore passage.

In, "Eyes of the Admiralty J.T. Serres : An Artist in the Channel Fleet 1799---1800" by M.K. Barritt, there is a picture of H.M.S. Unicorn [32 Guns] on patrol in the "Passage du Raz" and you can clearly see the Trépassér's Bay and the "Pointe du Raz". The great stretch of rocks known as "The Saints" can also be seen.

1115 Tevenez with its very distinctive white lighthouse on top is now abeam to Starboard. There is a gaff rigged vessel with a red mainsail on the horizon ahead. A yacht is motoring towards me coming the other way. You can now see right into the Baie de Trépassés and the houses and roads can be clearly seen.

1140 To my amazement 10 canoes are crossing my path directly ahead on course for the Île de Sein. My British friends have decided against the inshore passage and are now working their way back out. Eleven yachts can be seen in front of me.

1142 La Vielle is abeam. [11 minutes early which is within our limit of plus or minus 15 minutes!]. Four yachts are coming up astern.

1143 La Plate is abeam. Log 19.11. Altered course to round it.

1145 La Plate is in transit with la Vielle. Log 19.27. Increased revs to 1400. Speed through the water 5.2 knots. Speed over the ground 5.7 knots. Course 140(T). 22 miles to Cap Caval Buoy off Le Pointe de Penmarch.

1155 Pointe de Raz Lighthouse abeam to Port.

We have now rounded the Raz!!! Wind is Force 1 to 2 on the Starboard beam. A French fighter plane has just shrieked past on its way out to sea. The mainsail is just about filling.

1200 Log 20.66. 1400 revs. Speed through the water 5.3 knots. Speed over the ground 5.9 knots. Being overtaken by a French yacht close on my Starboard quarter. I'm also crossing the bows of a yacht which is beating to windward on the Starboard tack.

1210 Set staysail and jib. All 3 sails are now drawing with the wind abeam. Reduced revs to 1200. Speed through the water 5.2 knots. Speed over the ground 5.8 knots.

1230 Reduced revs to 1000. I think the wind has strengthened slightly. I hope so!!! It would be nice to sail. 4.6 knots through the water. 5.6 over the ground.

1245 have overtaken a Bavaria 31 which has stopped her engine and is trying to sail.

1300 Log 23.14. Course 135(T). Revs 1000. Wind on beam all 3 sails set. Speed through water 4.6. Speed over ground 5.3. A motor yacht is passing to Starboard going the other way. The town of Audienne can be clearly seen to Port although it is more than 5 miles away. A big fishing trawler called "Cheperion" is motoring past and kicking up a huge wake which sets the "Tarla" "hobbyhorsing" as she passes.

The bay of Audienne stretches away in a great loop with the coast eventually disappearing over the horizon. We have made good 7.2 miles in the last hour and a quarter and there is just under 15 miles to go to Cap Caval Buoy.

1310 A dolphin just surfaced crossing my bows. Very close indeed! Now there are several. I grab my camera and take photos, one after the other, hoping to catch their images.

1335 A speedboat is coming up on my Port quarter at a tremendous speed and just as I start getting worried that she had seen me she slows right down and turns towards the Pointe de Raz. I think now that it is actually a fishing boat!

1400 log 27.78. Revs 1000. Speed through the water 5.1. Speed over the ground 5.9. Altered course to Starboard 5 degrees to keep us on track for Cap Caval Buoy. There is a fishing boat ahead fine on the Port bow.

1402 Stopped engine. Speed through the water 4 knots. Speed over the ground 4.1. Passed the fishing boat close to Port. There is a yacht under engine coming towards me. The two towers on the Pointe de Penmarch can now be clearly seen but they appear to stick up straight out of the sea! Wind is from the West Force 3. I cannot believe that we are sailing at last after so much motoring. I'm keeping my fingers crossed!

1500 The engine has been stopped for an hour! Log 31.62. Speed through the water 4.5 knots. Speed over the ground 5.5 knots. Tarla has made good 4.8 miles over the ground in the last hour and 3.84 miles through the water.

It really is glorious to be sailing at last! A broad reach in a Force 3 with the sun shining. A blue sky and a blue sea. How wonderful! A sloop with a red hull has very slowly overhauled me in the last hour but my guess is that she is almost 40 feet long. Men Hir Tower [Black and White] can now be clearly seen on the Pointe de Penmarch as can the big lighthouse "Eckmühl" which is 213 feet high.

1512 There is a yacht coming directly towards me under power'

1515 She passed down my Port side. She is British and called the "Eowyn". I have just noticed a Wharram catamaran to Starboard with a gaff mainsail and jib. Looks like the Tiki 26. I am going to keep a close eye on her as she is about the same waterline length as the "Tarla" although much lighter. Cap Laval Buoy is now in sight fine on the port Bow.

The Wharram cat might be the Tiki 28 as she has some type of "pop-top" in the middle. She is faster than the "Tarla" by about 1 knot I think.

1537 Transit of Men Hir tower with Eckmühl lighthouse. Log 34.05. Speed through the water 3.9. Speed over the ground 4.3. I am being overtaken by a British sailing sloop coming up astern.

1605 Cap Caval Buoy abeam to port. Log 35.60. Set flat cut spinnaker. Furled jib. The "Tarla" now has 430 square feet of sail set. Wind now almost dead astern. Speed through the water 4.3 knots. Speed over the ground 4.5. There are a lot of fishing boats crossing my bow now going into Guilvinec. There appear to be 7 of them that will be crossing my course in the very near future all kicking up a huge wake which will set me rocking and knock the wind out of my sails!

Just past Guilvinec is the Port of Loctudy which leads to Pont L'Abbé. Pont L'Abbé is the self styled capital of Pays Bigouden [roughly the region between the river Odet and the Bay of Audienne). Port L'Abbé was founded by a monk from Loctudy who built the first bridge across the river estuary (hence the name). This monk also built the original castle in the 14th century.

In 1847 [about the same time as the Irish Famine] a riot broke out in Pont L'Abbé when potatoes were loaded onto a ship while the local people starved. Later, there were many strikes which arose because of the poor pay and conditions of the local lace-making industry. Potatoes again reared their head in 1961 when farmers demonstrated violently over the price being given for new potatoes.

The most famous element of the Bigouden culture is the traditional headdress worn by the women. It is said that the height of the headdress was increased after the Duke of Chaulnes had demolished the local bell towers, but this is legend. The "monument aux Bigoudens" built in Pont L'Abbe by F. Bazin in 1931, shows relatively small headdresses about 10 centimetres high. The headdresses seem to have grown after the Second World War but are hardly seen today, except in religious and traditional festivals.

1650 Lowered the spinnaker. Started engine. 1200 revs. Just the mainsail set. Speed through the water 5.0 knots. Speed over the ground 4.3 knots.

1655 Spineg buoy abeam to Port. Log 38.64. Wind aft. Just the mainsail set. Revs 1200. Speed through the water 5.0. Speed over the ground 4.5. Course 90(T).

1700 Log 39.00 Speed through the water 5.1. Speed over the ground 4.6. Course 90(T). 10 miles to go to a position off Rouge de Glénan. I am keeping a very sharp lookout for fishermen's buoys as they seem to be all around me and I have altered course for them several times.

1800 Karek Greis Buoy abeam to Port log 44.08. Speed through the water 4.9. Speed over the ground 5.2. Revs 1200. Just mainsail set with wind aft. Plotted position on the chart. Just 4.8 miles to go before we are abeam of Rouge de Glénan. The Îles de Glénan are now in sight on the horizon.

1815 A sloop under sail has crossed my bows heading for Bénodet. I am overhauling the Wharram cat which is to Starboard and is still under sail only. I am having to alter course for fishermen's buoys all the time.

Bénodet's position at the mouth of the Odet river has played a large part in shaping its history. Although the port is a 16th century construction it was previously, from the middle-ages on, an outer harbour for Quimper. Legend has it that the local fishermen hunted whales all the way to Newfoundland and thus discovered America before 1492! Its golden era only truly began in the 19th century when it became a significant seaside resort. Artists like Emile Zola, André Suarez, Eugène Boudin and Guillaume Apollinaire, to name but a few, flocked in.

On the opposite bank of the river Odet to Bénodet lies Sainte-Marine which is a charming fishing village and a much quieter resort than Bénodet. The two main attractions of this village are the 19th century fort and soldier's shelter. There are several chapels which date from the 16th century. The village's fishing thrived until the early 20th century when more than 300 fishermen earned their living here. Today there are just six fishing boats.

1830 I am abeam of the Wharram cat. Plotted position on chart.

1950 Dropped anchor off the Île de Pomfret which is now a lee shore in a Force 4 gusting 5. I have put out plenty of chain and I have a large anchor. Handed log [Reading 53.85]. I looked up the tidal range for the Île de Pomfret and found that it is 4.2 metres at Springs. As it is Neaps it will be less than this. I am currently anchored in 3.3 metres and so I should be OK with 25 metres of chain out.

The reason that the log records so little during the past hour and twenty minutes is because I had to take over the steering as in the rising wind the autopilot could not cope. It will be interesting to see if this wind eases at sunset! Meanwhile the young people from the École Voile Française are whizzing all around me in their Hobie cats.

It is very nice after a long day to sit here in the cabin sheltered from the wind even if it is leaping around. I am very lucky. In one sense these islands are like the Pacific Islands. Many would not know the difference except that there are no palm trees. When I was anchored here in the "Chang O" seven years ago I met this couple in a Maurice Griffith's designed "Golden Hind" 31 who were anchored close by. They very kindly invited me aboard for the evening and I spent one of the most memorable nights of my life mainly discussing Catholicism with them. Nine months later the woman died and Kevin now has a new partner. But I will never forget that evening here.

2200 A Hobie cat has capsized in front of me and the two young people on board her cannot right her in this strength of wind. Luckily for me a young lady in a rescue launch turned up and helped the two young men right her. In their capsized state they were slowly drifting down on me so I would probably have been able to help them from the "Tarla" anyway but I would not have been keen to pump up my dinghy and launch it in these conditions.

The sun is now sinking over the Western Horizon. It would be perfect to calculate an azimuth to correct our compass deviation!

The "Tarla" is extremely noisy in these conditions as each wave hits her under the bridge deck. It is probably rougher here at High water [which it almost is].

2230 The most beautiful sunset. Layers of pink clouds stacked one above the other over the low lying islands of Glénan. Nobody can accuse the "Tarla" of not knowing how to "hobbyhorse". Her two noses go up and down like a yo-yo!!!

2245 I put a riding light in the rigging and decided, because of the strength of the wind, that the battery operated one was the right choice. The paraffin hurricane lamp would have blown out in a moment. The wind has now shifted round and is coming directly from the direction of Concarneau. There is nothing to damp down the waves between there and here and the wind is still as strong! I am reminded of the ditty:

"There's a strange sort of up and down motion
That belongs to the treacherous ocean
And inspires me at once with the notion
I never was meant for the sea!"
[Anon].

Drunk a last whiskey in the "hobbyhorsing" cabin gently lit by my large paraffin lantern.

2300 Turned in.

11

ÎLES DE GLÉNAN
TO PORT TUDY, ÎLE DE GOIX

Les Îles de Glénan are a beautiful archipelago made up of an intricate mixture of islands fringed by sandy beaches, rocks and shoals. In character it resembles a miniature Scilly Islands and is the home of the Centre Nautique de Glénans (CNG), the largest sailing school in Europe, which gives young people training at all levels from basic seamanship to cruising and ocean racing. The school's main base is on the Île Çigogne but I can speak from experience of the huge number of hobie cats which take off from the Île de Pomfret which I am anchored off. The founding of this sailing school after the Second World War is a story in itself but I think it would be fair to say that it was part of the French determination to move forward and build a new and better World and thousands of French people (and Irish in Glénan's Irish bases) have benefited as a result.

The Glénans are very popular with day trippers as there are daily ferries from Loctudy, Bénodet, Concarneau and Beg-Meil. The boats arrive at the main island of St. Nicholas where there are a couple of restaurants as well as the international diving school and France's smallest nature reserve which was founded in 1974 to protect the Glénan Narcissus, the small white flower that carpets the island in April. Île de Pomfret is instantly recognised by its lighthouse and semaphore station while Île Çigogne can be identified by its fort which was built in 1756 to keep the English privateers out of the lagoon. The lagoon is renowned for the clarity of its water and the whiteness of its sand.

Wednesday 7ᵗʰ July, 2010.

0500 Got up and had a cup of tea. The wind has gone down. Almost a flat calm. There is a slight swell. It must have been quite rough last night because there are things that have fallen off the work surfaces in the galley which have never fallen off before. Part of the problem is that large fishing vessels drive past at speed kicking up a tremendous wash.

0630 Went back to bed. As it is now light I have doused the riding light.

0915 Got up again and had another cup of tea! Read my book.

0950 Did the washing up.

1000 Made out passage plan from Île de Pomfret to Port Tudy, Île de Goix. Total distance 22 miles.

1040 Started engine. Hauled anchor. Set mainsail and proceeded to sea.

1055 Île de Pomfret Lighthouse abeam to Starboard. Streamed log (Zeroed). Course 115 (T) for Car Loch Buoy. Distance 3.5 miles. Engine revs 1000. Speed through the water 3.9 knots. Speed over the ground 3.8. Wind East Force 1. There are 2 yachts close by to Port Motor Sailing. The sea is smooth with the slightest of swells. Car Loch Buoy can be seen straight ahead.

1100 Log 0.50 Course 115(T). Fast Motorboat is crossing my bow from Starboard to Port. As it comes closer I see that it is a French coastguard cutter.

1110 Speedboat passed to Starboard going the other way. Far away to Port I can see where Concarneau should be. I am reminded that its Breton name is "Konk Kerne" meaning "The Bay of Cornwall". I am also reminded of the fact that when I was Third Mate of the "Golden Comet", a motor refrigerated ship of 1,200 tons, we landed a full cargo of tuna fish in Concarneau in 1967. We had loaded these fish from the Concarneau fishermen who had sailed their boats down to Walvis Bay in South West Africa.

1115 Large Blue Cutter with sails furled crossing my stern obliquely heading for the Île de Pomfret.

1120 Fast Motorboat going the other way passed me to Port. It is a beautiful day with no clouds and a completely blue sky. What a contrast with the anchorage last night! The Breton coast is spread out as a panorama along my Port side. Fishing boats and sailing yachts motor-sailing can be seen in various directions.

1138 have just been overtaken by a large sailing yacht (40foot?) under power doing about 6 knots. She is full of people as usual and we all wave!

1148 Car Loch BRB Buoy abeam to Port. Log 3.41 miles. Altered course to 100(T) for Port Tudy outer buoy--- Speerbrecker. Distance 18 miles. Increased revs to 1200. Speed through the water 4.6 knots. Speed over the ground 4.8 knots. Île de Goix is already in sight although it is 15 miles away.

1200 Log 04.40. Course 100(T). Speed through the water 4.6 knots. Speed over the ground 4.8 knots.

1210 Jaune de Glénan East Cardinal Buoy abeam to Port. Log 04.96. Course 100(T).

1300 Log 08.63. Course 100(T). Speed through the water 4.8. Revs 1200. Course 100(T). Plotted Tarla's position on the chart.

The sea is the most gorgeous blue. The sun beats down. The land in the hazy distance looks a light green with brown rocks and little dots which are houses. Le Île de Pomfret is just disappearing astern. Le Île de Goix is becoming much clearer and I can see Lorient on the mainland. We have 12 miles to go!

Away in the haze to Port is the entrance to the Aven river leading to Pont Aven. "Pont Aven, ville de renom, 14 moulins, 15 maisons" [Pont Aven renouned for its 14 mills and 15 houses]. There are more than 15 houses now but this must have seemed to be the case to the artist Gauguin when he first visited his "petit trou pas cher" in 1886. A "cheap little hole" was exactly what this impecunious artist was looking for at the time.

1310 Yellow Special Purpose Buoy abeam to Starboard. Log 09.36. Course 100(T). There is a sailing yacht crossing ahead (about 1 mile) under power. She has a big white awning over her boom rigged like a tent. I wonder how they see out at the sides!

1330 Can just see the lighthouse on the Île de Pomfret but nothing else. The land on which it stands is below the horizon. We are exactly 12 miles from it.

1350 A large French catamaran has just passed to Port going the other way. She is under power with her mainsail set. I have also just passed a fishing boat to Starboard. She is stopped while tending her buoys.

1400 log. 13.07. Course 100(T). Speed through the water 4.8 knots. Speed over the ground 5.2. Revs 1200 plus the mainsail. Plotted position on the chart and discovered that the "Tarla" has made good 5 miles in the last hour. There are 7 miles still to go to Port Tudy outer buoy. Wind now NE Force 1.

1415 A school of dolphins have surrounded Tarla [5 of them] but they only stayed a minute before swimming off. A huge trimaran is tacking in the distance near Pen Men headland on the Île de Goix. A fast motorboat is crossing the horizon to Starboard. Each of the noses of the trimaran appear to be orange with the rest of the hull green. Her sails are the usual "dirty" colour that "high tech" sails are now-days. By 1440 I could see that the top of her mainsail was orange with a "3" on it in white and each of her three orange noses also has a white "3" on them. "Groupnama is written on the "dirty" part of her mainsail and on the green part of her hull. She is in fact "Groupnama 3" registered in Lorient and representing the "cutting edge" of French technology. She is 31.50 metres long and weighs only 18 tonnes. She is thus light but with only moderate sail area, equipped with an open cockpit and very spartan accommodation. She was considered to be the fastest of the pretenders for the Jules Verne Trophy provided that the wind stayed below 20 knots. The theory being that on a circumnavigation the wind is only stronger than this for 20% of the time. Therefore being the fastest in under 20 knots of wind will produce the winning formula. This was the philosophy of Franck Cammas and his team who created her. And it is the philosophy which saw Groupama 3 win the Jules Verne Trophy.

I looked up Groupama 3 on the web and discovered that on Wednesday the 7th of July Franck Cammas set out from Lorient on his own aboard this huge vessel to perform the qualifier for the Route du Rhum race to the West Indies. He returned to Lorient on the evening of Sunday the 11th having covered 1,500 nautical miles. He said "During the four days at sea, I didn't have to deal with any gales. However, I did have to put in a lot of manoeuvres as the wind was very shifty". Questioned about his ability to single-hand a vessel designed for a crew of 10 Franck seemed pleasantly surprised. "Certain manoeuvres like gybing or furling the gennaker are very physical and above all very long. As such you always have to correctly anticipate how things are going to pan out so you don't end up in a tight corner, especially when the wind picks up".

On deck the layout has been considerably revised since Groupama 3 won the Jules Verne Trophy. The lone crew member is now able to use the strength of his legs when operating the winches. "The bicycle idea isn't entirely novel as its already been used on America's Cup boats some 30 or so years ago. Aboard Groupama 3, the bike enables me to alternate between working my arms and working my legs. As a result I lose less time during manoeuvres" says Franck. For those interested there is a great deal more on the web!

1450 Pen Men Lighthouse (Black and White stripes) is abeam to Starboard. Log 16.70. Course 100(T). There is a small warship [A751] approaching me from ahead. She passed down my Starboard side. She is obviously French but is not flying an ensign so I did not dip mine but waved instead!

1453 Altered course 10 degrees to Starboard to head for Speerbrecker East Cardinal Buoy off Port Tudy. Distance 2.478 miles according to the chartplotter.

1500 Log 17.54. Course 120(T). Speed through the water 4.8 knots. Speed over the ground 5.1. Revs 1200. Wind SW Force 1. The big tri is passing astern of me. It is amazing how fast she is in almost no wind. Her mainsail is reefed 50% and she has only a medium size headsail up. Two sloops are also beating to windward very slowly going in the opposite direction to me. So the wind must be NW and it is only my speed under power which is making it seem to be SW! The concrete breakwater of Port Tudy is now in sight. I can see 12 yachts around me mostly drifting under sail but a few under power.

1520 Abeam of the harbour entrance to port Tudy. Hauled log [Reading 19.01]. Swung round into the wind and lowered mainsail and then proceeded into Port Tudy. Imagine my surprise when I looked at the chartplotter and saw a ship transmitting on AIS [which is compulsory for ships of over 300 tonnes]. I was fascinated because it was not the ferry but a vessel called the "Sea Quest" which turned out to be a Halberg Rassey 53 whose wealthy owner had invested in an AIS transponder.

1540 Tied up to mooring buoys in Port Tudy. Tidied up and had lunch. Helped tie up the yachts that rafted up alongside me. The French yacht on my starboard side belongs to a young couple. He is the Chief Officer of a large Tug. He is aged about 30. Apparently being a French firm he works 7 weeks on and 7 weeks off. She has just finished a degree in Geography and has not yet got a job. After they both went ashore in their dinghy I sent the usual texts concerning my safe arrival and then I retired for a "snooze".

1830 Got up. Poured myself a glass of wine and was just about to drink it when the couple next door invited me for rum and lemon! After talking to them for about an hour I returned to Tarla, cooked a meal and drunk the wine. Read a book and worked out the passage plan for Étel.

During my hours conversation with the couple next door I learned that they had sailed from St.Malo which is their home Port. He is one of six children. She comes from the Breton coast from a fishing village called L'Aberdulit. Their boat was bought cheap because it hasn't an engine. They use an outboard motor and carry 10 litres of fuel. The outboard is old but he says that it is easy to repair because you can lift it off and take it to bits in the cockpit. Recently they sprung a leak because the keel started to come off and so they had to be lifted ashore in Vannes. Once ashore he heavily reinforced the bottom with fibreglass. The boat is a Swedish design but very lightly constructed and so she is fast under sail. She is about 30 feet long.

2200 Anne Phoned.

2300 Turned in.

12
PORT TUDY, ÎLE DE GOIX
TO ÉTEL

Thursday the 8ᵗʰ of July, 2010.

0830 Got up to discover that everything was shrouded in thick fog. Had a cup of tea and prayed that the fog would go away soon!

I look at the many yachts jammed into the harbour and reflect that there were once as many fishing boats. Port Tudy was France's main centre for Tuna fishing from 1840 until 1940 and it is all documented in their museum. Indeed, the museum traces the island's history from the Bronze-Age to the present time. About half a mile up the hill from Port Tudy is Goix's main village and the church there has a tuna fish on top of its bell tower. Another interesting fact is that the inhabitants of Goix are known as "Groisillons"!

0915 I think that the fog is starting to clear as the sun is just beginning to shine through it.

0930 The fog has indeed cleared. I have just paid the boy in the boat 13 Euro which appears to be a flat charge for an 8 metre boat.

0955 Cast off from the mooring buoys in Port Tudy. Had to jill around while the ferry departed ahead of me.

1015 Speerbrecker East Cardinal Buoy abeam. Set course of 095(T) for Roheu South Cardinal Buoy off Étel. Distance 8 miles. Revs 1000. Speed through the water 4.3 knots. Speed over the ground 4.7. Wind NW Force 1. Sunny and Hot with excellent visibility. There are yachts motoring all around me some with their mainsails set.

1030 Three small fishing boats are close by. One of them is crossing my bow as is a sailing yacht under power. The fishing boat that I have just passed close by cannot be more than 16 feet long with 2 big men in her. She has a small cabin and an outboard motor.

1055 there is a yacht motor-sailing crossing my bow from Port.

1100 Log 3.04. Course 095(T). Stopped engine and set all 3 sails. I am too early for the recommended 1½ hours before high water to get over the bar into Étel so I might as well drift!

Away to Port is the great port of Lorient. Lorient is Brittany's fourth largest city. It lies in an immense natural harbour which is protected from the Atlantic Ocean by the Île de Goix. It was once a key base for French colonialism, and was the home to the Campagnie des Indes, an equivalent to the Dutch and English East India Companies, which was founded in the mid 17th century. During the Second World War Lorient was a major target for the Allies as the 'U' boat pens were housed here. Since the war the French have expanded some of them and used them for their nuclear submarines. Others provide a tourist attraction.

Between the first Friday and the second Sunday of August Lorient is host to a very large Celtic Festival. It is during these 10 days that the town is at its most lively.

1115 All the yachts around me are completely becalmed, just as I am. There is just enough wind to make the "Tarla" point in the right direction at almost zero knots! At least the sails provide me with shade and its very peaceful. According to my calculations I should not arrive at the bar until 1330 and as I am only about 6 miles away I have plenty of time.

1125 A big RIB full of people has just roared past me going the other way and the "Tarla" rocks heavily in their wake. My guess is from watching the seaweed floating past that the "Tarla" is making about ¼ of a Knot.

1135 Another RIB with only one person on it has just belted by. A yacht motoring with no sail set has just crossed my stern. I think that there is only one man on her.

1200 I have just dropped an apple core into the water at the bow and timed it until it reached the stern. It took 23 seconds to cover a distance of 26 feet! There is a yacht with her mainsail set crossing my stern. Log 3.08. Course 095(T). I plotted the "Tarla's" position on the chart. Distance still to go to Etel bar 4.7 miles. There is a motor cruiser passing down my Port side. 4.7 miles will take about an hour and 10 minutes at 4 knots. Therefore start engine at 1215.

1205 Another yacht motoring with no sail set is crossing my bow from Starboard.

1210 A sloop with both sails set and engine running has just crossed my stern from Port.

1215 Started the engine. Revs 1000. Log 3.10. Course 095(T). Speed through the water 4.4 knots. Speed over the ground 4.1. Both the main and the jib are filling and therefore contributing something, however small, to our forward motion.

1230 Small Coaster/Dredger passing astern in the distance [From Port to Starboard]. Altered course to 105(T) to give the rocks round Roheu a wide berth. Log 4.40.

1300 Roheu Tower[Yellow/Black] abeam to Port. No sign of the South Cardinal Buoy!!! Log 6.45. Revs 1000. Course 105(T). Speed through the water 5.0 knots. Speed over the ground 5.0 knots. The wind is slightly stronger---maybe Force 2!

1302 Altered course to 90(T). Two sailing yachts can be seen coming out of Étel ahead. A fishing boat is passing me on the Port side going the other way at speed. Furled sails, put out fenders and mooring lines on both sides.

1330 Crossed the Étel bar. Minimum depth recorded 3.9 metres.

1400 Tied up in Étel harbour. Unfortunately bashed some paint off the Port rudder trying to back her into a berth which was upwind of me. No real harm, just scratched paint! Wind got me but I have no real excuses. I could have done it better. I went to the Capitanerie and after a great deal of calculation on the computer, which I could have done much quicker in my head, he decided that I owed 42 Euro for two nights stay [This was based on a formula whereby the length of the boat was multiplied by the width]. Showers were included in the price.

1545 The Vion Weather Station says that it is raining!!! The sun beats down from a cloudless blue sky!!! Humidity outside 77% Temp 27.1 C. Inside the cabin it is 57% and 27.1 C.

1930 The Temperature outside is 32.9 C. [Humidity 22%]. Inside the cabin the Temperature is 27.8 C. [Humidity 47%].

I have just come back from a walk round the town where my friend Peter Spry-Leverton rang me to see how I was getting on. I purchased a baguette and now propose to eat it with cheese and pâté for supper with, of course, the usual red wine. I feel full of apprehension as to whether this is really a good place to leave the "Tarla" for the Winter---it seems somewhat exposed---and, secondly, whether I will be allowed to leave her here---they may be full up. However, I draw strength from the fact that in situations like this Almighty God has never yet let me down.

2030 Went for another walk.

2230 Turned in.

What is so striking about Étel is the clear blue water and the extensive golden sand. The town itself has a pedestrian precinct and many restaurants. It appeared to me to specialise in "bric-a-brac" shops. Obviously everything is very tourist orientated. The problems of getting in and out over the bar where the stream can run at more than 6 knots is challenging. What I had not expected was that the harbour would be full of fast motor cruiser type fishing boats which can presumably be trailed away for the Winter. With their speed the rate of the stream is of little consequence provided they tackle it in fine weather. When I had decided on Étel as my final destination it was based on the website concerning the harbour which said that there were 360 sheltered berths and that it would not be crowded as most yachtsmen would not like the bar. Obviously I was wrong but without visiting a place in advance it is very difficult to form a true impression. This line of thinking is already raising the spectre of having come so far and having nowhere to go!

The strong streams in Étel are caused by an inland sea which fills and drains with each tide. This sea known as La Mer d'Étel can unfortunately no longer be entered by masted vessels as a bridge known as Le Pont Lorois has been built just above the town. The bridge is said to have a clearance of 9 metres and at Spring tides the current flowing under it can reach 10 knots! However, above this bridge is an ancient oratory at St. Cado which would be well worth a visit if you had a suitable dinghy with a powerful outboard motor. I donn't!

13
ÉTEL
TO HOUAT

Friday the 9ᵗʰ of July, 2010.

0630 Got up and had a cup of tea. On tenterhooks not knowing whether the "Tarla" can stay here for the year.

0750 Went for a shower.

0830 Had another cup of tea.

0910 Went to the Capitainerie and discovered that there is a 3 year waiting list for permanent berths in Étel. Decided to move on to explore the possibilities of staying for the Winter on the River Vilaine which leads up to Redon.

From 0910 until 1200 did some hard thinking! Where was I going to go? After 500 miles and 2 months away I was more than ready to go home to Ireland and see Anne and my children. I had visions of sailing round for ever looking for a place to stay for the Winter with nowhere to go! I rang Anne and told her what was happening and that I had decided to try my luck in the Vilaine.

I also rang my son Niall and asked him to carry out a search on the possibility of finding a berth for the Winter on the Vilaine. I also sent texts to my daughter Aoife and to Peter Spry-Leverton informing them of the situation.

Niall got back to me to say that the best bet seemed to be a place called Foleux or Redon. I will try them in that order.

1230 Went shopping and discovered that everything had closed for lunch!

1405 Cast off from the pontoon in Étel harbour.

1430 I am over the bar! Despite making 6 knots through the water I was at times only making 2.9 knots over the ground. Engine Revs 1800. The wind is Force 4 Forward of the beam. At least the tide and wind are more or less in the same direction otherwise the seas over the bar would be much worse than they are. On the way out of the river I passed a Wharram Pahi 31 Catamaran with a lot of young French people on her coming in. We all waved to each other.

1440 Hoisted Mainsail and set the Staysail and Jib. Stopped the engine. Streamed the log [Zeroed]. The "Tarla" is hard on the wind making a steady 6 knots through the water [5 knots over the ground]. In the gusts the speed goes up to 6.9 knots for several minutes at a time. This is sailing! Going to windward at almost 7 knots is bouncy but she hardly slams. Occasionally a dollop of spray reaches the cockpit but not a lot.

1505 Pierre Noires abeam to Port. Log 1.48. Course 160(T). Wind now on the beam. Speed through the water 6.4 knots. Speed over the ground 5.9 knots. With the wind on the beam the "Tarla" is "running on rails" at a steady 6.5 knots. No spray. Little movement with the occasional slight lurch when she meets a bigger than expected sea. From this point on I had to take over and hand-steer. Left to the autopilot the "Tarla" kept coming round hard on the wind with no reduction in speed but with the autopilot "squeaking" because it couldn't cope.

I was now rounding the Quiberon Peninsular which juts out nine miles into the sea and is 22 metres wide at its narrowest point. Port Maria used to be France's principal sardine fishing port and it still has around 200 fishing boats. St. Pierre Quiberon is the peninsula's main village and the Battle of Quiberon Bay was fought off its Eastern shore in 1759. There amongst the rocks the Royal Navy beat the French and the latter suffered their worst ever defeat.

With the Quiberon peninsular to Port away to Starboard were the distant shores of Brittany's largest island---Belle Île.

There was a time when it was under British occupation. Arriving in its main town Le Palais the first thing you will notice is the star shaped Citadelle Vauban, which was built by the famous military engineer Vauban in the 18ᵗʰ century. Belle Île was occupied by British troops from 1761 to 1763 before being handed back in exchange for Menorca. In the North West, where we are now opposite, is the attractive fishing village of Sauzôn which dries out at low water. It was here that the first canneries were opened in 1843. The Northernmost point of Belle Île is interesting because there is a small lighthouse and a fort. The fort was purchased by the great actress Sarah Bernhardt and she lived there from 1894.

1628 Le Pouilloux Cardinal Buoy abeam to Port. Log 09.70. [An average speed through the water of just over 6 knots in the last hour and twenty three minutes].

1710 Goue Vaz Sud abeam.

On the horizon to Port is the Gulfe du Morbihan. Morbihan is rich in megalithic sites, nowhere more so than Locmariaquer. Here you will find Le Grand Menhir which is now on the ground in four pieces. This is the largest stone ever erected in pre-historic Europe as far as we know. The island of Gavrin is in the Gulf and probably represents the most impressive megalithic sight in Brittany. There is a long stone passageway adorned with carvings and its tumulus is similar in shape and age (3500BC) to Egypt's pyramids. The largest local settlement is the medieval town of Vannes. At the other end of the Golf is the town of Auray where Benjamin Franklin landed from North America on the 3ʳᵈ of December 1776 in his quest to raise money for the war of independence of the breakaway British Colonies. He had to deal with the French government in the form of Louis XVI! My hero Bernard Moitessier, the great single-handed French sailor, is buried in the village of Le Bono close by.

On the East side of the Golfe du Morbihan lies the 14ᵗʰ Century Château de Suscino which was a former hunting lodge of the Dukes of Brittany. From 1471 until 1483 this castle was home to the exiled Henry Tudor (later Henry VII of England) during the English Wars of the Roses.

1830 Hauled log reading 21.40. This means that Tarla has averaged 5.6 knots through the water since I stopped the engine 3 hours 50 minutes ago.

1900 Anchored in Treac'her Goured off the East end of Île Houat. The beach is like a Caribbean island but at the moment it has decided to blow Force 6 so I cannot enjoy it so much!

What I did enjoy today was sailing the whole way. Her speedometer never dropped below 5 knots and was touching 7 at times. This was beating, reaching and running. A really good sail. The downside was that I had to steer because the auto-pilot could not cope when beam reaching or running. As I was steering I wasn't able to write so much in the log as usual. But I did pass a number of yachts! One of which was a big one, a ketch with her mizzen furled, going the other way with her lee rail well under. I had to alter course for several of these yachts as they had the right of way. The "Tarla" was sailing fastest at the beginning and end of her passage. For much of the long run down to Houat she was making 5 knots with the wind aft and a following sea. She remained easy to steer at all times and has very good directional stability. A decent autopilot should certainly be able to cope. The search begins!

I am delighted to say that the "Tarla" doesn't sheer about any more than the big mono-hulls while she is at anchor in this strong wind. I presume this is because she is riding to 25 metres of 8mm chain but I am not using a bridle---the chain leads straight over the bow roller in the centre of the foredeck. The 15kg Delta Anchor does seem to work extremely well. I notice with great interest that the RNLI use them.

Coming into the bay under mainsail, staysail and heavily reefed jib the "Tarla" was making 5.4 knots through the water hard on the wind in a Force 6, gusting 7. However, as she was in the lee of the land she was not having to face any appreciable sea. Nevertheless, the tops of the small waves were being torn off by the wind in the squalls. I was getting quite wet!

I was also delighted that the mainsail came down so easily---the direct result of using copious quantities of WD 40 on the sail slides. I was also very pleased to find that when I furled the jib and staysail that the "Tarla" "weather-cocked" into the wind and only fell off when I lowered the main. This is a useful safety feature.

In a strong wind my seaman's instinct is to be concerned. I can never relax. Strong wind is a problem!

Of course a fair wind or a wind like today that gives one such wonderful sailing is one of God's gifts. But equally strong winds could mean dragging anchors and being blown onto rocks or dragging onto another yacht especially in such a crowded anchorage as this. It makes you forever vigilant and I still feel this sense of unease when I am tucked up in bed in a house on land when the wind blows strongly even though I know logically that nothing can happen. One's early training counts and one's instincts have been honed to a fine edge.

I have just counted 75 yachts anchored here.

Houat is a strangely shaped island about 2 miles long (In Breton Houat means Duck). At its Eastern end there are long promontories. En Tal on the NE is low; the Southern one is higher, with off-lying rocks. Between these headlands lie the remarkable sands of Treac'her Goured where I am now anchored. The old Port of Er Beg is on my Port beam as I lay head to the wind facing directly into the bay. This Port was destroyed by a tempest in 1951. The new harbour, Port St. Gildas, lies to the West of En Tal.

One of the things that make Houat famous is the asparagus which grows wild. It is a protected species as it can only be found here and on Portugal's Algarve and nowhere else. The other thing that makes Houat remarkable apart from its beautiful sandy and attractive coves is the "Eclosarium" which is a museum that explores the world of phytoplankton, the marine organism that is responsible for 80% of the World's oxygen.

Port St. Gildas is named after St Gildas de Rhuys, a 6th Century British Missionary who established a monastery near the entrance to the Morbihan. St. Gildas died in 570 when visiting Houat, and in accordance with his wishes his body was placed in a boat and pushed out to sea. Two months later, on the 11th March, the boat was washed ashore at what is now the entrance to Crouesty Marina close to the mouth of the Morbihan. Almighty God had taken him home! A chapel was built at the spot and it can still be seen on the South side of the Marina entrance at Crouesty. It has of course been rebuilt several times as in its exposed position it has suffered severe storm damage at times. Its history is recorded on a plaque by the porch.

2220 As the sun sinks the wind is dropping. Thank God! The Wharram catamaran (Tiki 28) that I was in company with coming up to the Île de Glénan is anchored two yachts along from me. Interestingly, she is flying the French flag as was the Wharram Pahi 31 which I passed coming out of the Étel river.

14

ÎLE DE HOUAT
TO THE PORT OF FOLEUX

Saturday the 10th of July.

0500 Got up and had a cup of tea. Watched the sun come up over the horizon and took a photo.

0630 Went back to bed again.

0820 Got up again and had another cup of tea. What a contrast with last night! It is warm and sunny with a gentle breeze. The wind has swung round from the WSW to the NNE.

0930 Hauled the anchor. Hoisted the Mainsail. Waved to the young couple in the Wharram cat who tried to speak to me but I couldn't hear them because of the noise of the engine. Headed out to sea. Course 070(T). Speed through the water 4.2 knots. Speed over the ground 3.9 knots. Engine Revs 1000.

0940 Streamed Log [Zeroed}.

0955 Set the two headsails. Speed through the water 4.4 knots. The sails are not flapping so they must be helping a bit!!!

1000 Log 00.00. Forgot to switch it on! Have now done so. There is a fishing vessel abeam to Port. There is also a yacht on a reciprocal course going the other way and passing down my Port side. Speed through the water and over the ground 4.4 knots. Engine revs 1000 plus mainsail, staysail and jib.

1010 Recherché West Cardinal Buoy in sight broad on the Port bow. I think I can see Locmariaquer Buoy slightly finer on the port bow in the hazy distance.

1020 Yacht crossing ahead under power from Starboard to Port.

1030 The wind has dropped completely. Furled Jib.

1043 Recherché West Cardinal Buoy [Yellow and Black] abeam to Port. Log 2.80. Course 68(T). Sails slatting. Flat calm. Warm sun. Blue sky. Blue sea. Temperature outside 27.3 C. Humidity 44%.

1052 I have just seen a huge jellyfish floating along the side of the "Tarla" to Port. Yesterday, when I was hand-steering in quite big waves I thought I had almost hit an unidentified object in the water. I now realise that it was almost certainly a jellyfish!

1100 Log 3.80. Course 068(T) Revs 1000 plus mainsail and staysail. Speed through the water 4.3 knots. Speed over the ground 4.6 knots. I plotted the "Tarla's" position on the chart and discovered that she had made good 4.3 miles in the last hour. There is a yacht motor-sailing, passing me to Port, going the other way. Another yacht is crossing ahead from Port to Starboard. Another one, even further ahead, is crossing the other way.

1110 Locimariaquer Buoy abeam to Port [Black and Red with two black balls on top]. Log 4.43. Course 068(T).

Just been passed by a small inflatable with 2 men in it. There are big wheels sticking up over the stern which can be lowered to pull it up a beach. Presumably it is on a fishing expedition but is currently 4.5 miles from land.

1115 There is fast fishing boat crossing my bow from Starboard to Port at speed.

1137 I have just crossed the bow of a yacht attempting to sail. She is on my Port side. Looking all round the horizon I can count 25 yachts either attempting to sail or motor-sailing.

1145 A yacht under sail going the other way passed quite close to my Starboard side.

1152 Another yacht under sail passes to Starboard. How do they manage to sail so well in so little wind?

1158 Another yacht passes to Starboard going the other way.

1200 Log 07.90. Course 070(T). Revs 1000. Speed through the water 4.2 knots. Speed over the ground 4.5. A speedboat is crossing my bows from Starboard to Port. Plotted the "Tarla's" position on the chart. She has made good 4.4 miles in the last hour.

Les Mats buoy is 5 miles distant ahead. A two-masted lugger is away on my Starboard bow sailing out to sea. A large yacht, which appears to be sailing, is crossing my bows going the other way. My sails continue to slat so they cannot be getting much wind or anywhere very fast!

There is supposed to be a yellow special purpose buoy fine on my Port bow about ¼ mile away according to the chart-plotter [But not my paper chart] but I cannot see it.

I've found it! The special purpose buoy looks like a fishing boat with a black hull and yellow/cream superstructure.

1220 Slowed down to let a yacht under sail pass ahead of me from Port to Starboard.

1225 Yellow special purpose buoy abeam to Port. Log 09.54. Course 070(T). Wind is now coming very gently from astern. ie: West. Force 2. I have let out the mainsail but I don't think that there is much point in setting the jib because it will be blanketed by the main as the staysail presently is. It is warm! Temperature outside 31.7 C. Humidity 37%. Île Dument can clearly be seen on the Starboard beam. A fast fishing boat is crossing my stern from Starboard.

1240 Another fishing boat is crossing my stern from Starboard and a yacht up ahead is crossing my bow from Starboard and another yacht is heading the other way on my Starboard beam.

1253 A speedboat has just crossed my bows from Port going very fast. I waved to them and they waved back. A yacht is passing to Starboard going the other way under power. A small fishing speedboat is also passing to Starboard going the other way.

1300 Log 12.20. Course 070(T). Revs 1000. Speed through

the water 4.5 knots. Speed over the ground 5.0 knots. Wind directly aft Force 2. Mainsail and staysail set.

1310 Les Mats Buoy Abeam to Port. Log 12.98. Course 050(T). I am heading for the green marker in the river entrance. Having consulted the chart and the Pilot I conclude that when "Basse der Keyroyal" is abeam to Port I should turn East for the river entrance with green and red buoys to guide me in. What I should not do is to try and go round the green marker that I am heading for as it is firmly ashore!

1330 "Basse der Keyroyal" abeam to Port. Altered course for entrance buoys. Hauled log reading 14.72.

1400 Passed between the two entrance buoys to the river. Stopped the engine. The depth over the bar was 3.7 metres at what must have been about half tide.

Had the most beautiful sail up the river at between 3 and 4 knots under main and staysail only. I lowered the main and furled the staysail just before the dam.

According to the 'Pilot':

"La Vilaine River is very pretty. It meanders through meadows, or between rush-covered banks or rocky cliffs. There is a dam at Arzal with a large lock. But this dam is not part of a hydroelectric scheme like the Rance in North Brittany. It is rather about the controlled drainage of the river and hence the changes in level in the lock are nothing like as great as near St. Malo. Now-days little commercial traffic uses the river. It is mostly devoted to holyday makers and yachts. There are sizeable Marina's at Arzal and La Roche Bernard. Yachts do not normally go beyond the latter which is 7 kilometres above the dam. Above this the river is much quieter. Port Foleux is 7 kilometres above la Roche Bernard at the old ferry crossing and a further 34 kilometres brings masted yachts to the town of Redon where they can enter the Breton canal system provided that they are of shallow draft and can take their mast down."

1530 Entered the lock and tied up to the vertical chains.

There is an obvious skill to this lock-work!

1600 Exited the lock.

1730 After sailing under jib only for 7 kilometres without the engine we rounded a corner in the river and came upon La Roche Bernard with many yachts moored on both sides of the river and two very tall bridges just upstream. It is easy to see why it has "Roche" in its name as a huge rock sticks up out of the land beside the old harbour which is an inlet off the main river. This ancient town was founded by Bernhardt, a Viking Chief, who realised its strategic importance as a port. According to the guide book of particular attraction, apart from its church and old houses are the maritime museum and "La Maison de L'Abeille" which explores the life of the bee. Apparently, it has a shop which sells honey. I will have to come back and find out at a future date!

1900 After a further beautiful sail under jib only through wooded rocky passes and meadowland for another 7 kilometres I tied up to a pontoon at Port Foleux next to another Heavenly Twins catamaran. She is one year younger than the "Tarla" and is owned by a French couple. She is called the "Val D'Agon".

2115 Sitting here in the cockpit as the sun sinks and the heavily wooded shores become darker it is difficult to think of a more beautiful or safer place. Unlike the sea one is unlikely to die here. I have hope that I will find a berth here and that this place in the middle of nowhere will become part of me. The chap in the Heavenly Twins astern of me is laying up here for the Winter for a total cost of 500 Euro. I am sure it will cost me more but I will be so pleased to have found such a beautiful home.

I watch closely as an old man works on his Wharram Tane catamaran which has no mast and has been fitted with very short beams and an outboard motor. He takes a cushion from his van and locks the van. He walks 10 paces and throws the cushion onto the catamaran. The cushion falls into the water. He retrieves it and climbs aboard the catamaran to make sure that it is securely lodged. He returns to his van and unlocks it. He has never been more than 10 paces from the van!

Tonight is such a contrast with last night when I turned in all standing because I was worried that the anchor might drag. It didn't and the 15kg Delta must be one of my best investments. I have a theory that with anchors it is weight that counts just as waterline length determines one's speed unless your boat is of ultra-light displacement.

A man has just come up to me and said that his mother was from Malahide in Dublin and how wonderful it was to see the Irish flag.

The French man from the other Heavenly Twins has just visited me and given me a quotation from the yard across the water which is called "La Cale de Neptune". They will crane you out, charge you by the month for the rent of their land, and crane you back in. Total cost E 156.74 + E 88.74 + E 60.75 per month. I do hope that there isn't a waiting list.

Sunday the 11ᵗʰ of July, 2010.

0730 Got up and had a cup of tea.

Talked to my new friend on the other Heavenly Twins and compared differences between our two vessels.

0900 Launched dinghy and spent about an hour getting the outboard to go. In the process I developed a blister on my right index finger through pulling the starter cord! This is the first time since last Summer that I have used the outboard. Anyway success at last and it now starts "first pull".

1030 My new friends in the heavenly Twins left for Sauzôn on Belle Ile.

1130 After a cup of coffee I crossed the river in the dinghy [with the outboard motor propelling it] and explored Foleux. There are no shops and there are only about 20 houses and one of them is boarded up and another one is for sale. The only service being offered to the visitor in the food and drink line is the Bar/Cafe at the water's edge. I discovered that "La Cale de Neptune" doesn't open until 1400 hrs on a Monday. This is probably because they are open on Saturday morning. Nobody has been near me so far and I don't think that the Capitainerie on my side of the river ever opens. The Capitainerie on the Foleux side do all the administration but of course as it was lunch time they were closed. Anne rang, but like last night we were cut off. I don't know if this is bad reception at this end or her end.

1330 Just had a charming conversation with the French couple who have moored up behind me. They are from Normandy and have kept their boat here for the last 10 years. They wanted to know what the flag was that the "Tarla" was flying. When I told them that it was Irish they expressed much surprise and said that they had never seen the Irish flag before!

Had a snooze.

Woken up by a fellow from the Capitainerie. I paid him for 2 nights---last night and tonight. He charged Euro 21 per night based on the Tarla's breadth and length. Total 42 Euro. He told me that there is a waiting list for an annual contract with the Marina of about 3 years but that a 6 month contract is much more easily come by.

1530 Went and had a very nice shower.

1540 The fellow from the Capitainerie returned and handed me 14 Euro as he said that he had miscalculated my fee. I thanked him for being so honest. This means that it costs 14 Euro per night for the "Tarla" to tie up to a pontoon here in the high season.

1600 Talked at length to the wife of the couple who came from Normandy in the yacht moored ahead of me. She pointed out that shopping was easily done from Foleux by taking the boat to La Roche Bernard which being 7 kilometres by river took about an hour. She also informed me that she and her husband had 3 weeks holiday in 2 weeks time and would be sailing to la Rochelle and back. Next year they want to go to the Scilly Islands.

I also had a lengthy talk with a fellow whose yacht was ashore in the boatyard. She is an Alan Hill designed cutter and was rigged by Sailspar of Brightlingsea in Essex [as is the "Tarla"]. His boat has been in this yard for the past 3 years and he and his wife are from near Durham in the North of England. He was very interested in my staysail arrangement and is thinking of duplicating it on his own boat.

1930 Cooked supper, drank wine, read book.

2130 Talked to an English couple whose son was in the Royal Navy.

2200 Turned in.

It rained heavily during the night.

Monday the 12 of July, 2010.

0730 Got up and had a cup of tea.

0830 Did the washing up.

0900---1130 Washed all my dirty clothes and hung them up to dry.

1130---1230 Filled up the water tanks. I am praying that I will be able to fix up Winter storage this afternoon. A great weight will be lifted off my mind if I can pull it off. I want to go home to Ireland and see Anne and my children. Two months seem to have been a very long time to have been estranged from them.

1400 I waited on the doorstep of "La Cale de Neptune" for them to open! They refused to take a deposit but were adamant that there would not be a problem of lifting Tarla out in September/October. I then hung around until the Capitainerie opened at 1500 after their lunch break.

From the Belgian lady in the Capitainerie who spoke excellent English I gathered that I could have a contract to stay until the end of August. I signed this and it cost E 118. Again worked out on the basis of length times breadth. The problem is that everybody comes back at the end of August when their holidays finish and thus there is a dearth of places. The solution may be to get myself lifted out at the beginning of September.

I was also told that seasonal contracts were agreed in early September for the coming year and that it was necessary to be there in early September to sort them out. Apparently the marina's policy is to allocate 70% of the places in the marina and on the mooring buoys to annual contracts and the remaining 30% go to people who have short term contracts or to visitors.

I owe the Belgian lady a lot because she showed me the light at the end of the tunnel. This was a great relief! She also ordered a taxi for me to pick me up from the Capitainerie at 0600 on Wednesday and take me to the railway station in Redon.

I then rang Niall up in Cork and got him to book me a railway ticket from Redon to London via Lille by TGV and Eurostar. Niall also booked me a flight back to Cork from Stansted which I could use after I had visited my Father. The cost of making travel arrangements like this is considerable [£205 from Redon to London for example] but given that I didn't know when I could leave until today it is a necessary cost which hopefully will not be repeated in the future.

1600 I left the visitor' pontoon and moved to my designated buoy which is in a small river that joins the Vilaine at Foleux. I then lowered and bagged the staysail and jib. There is no point in them sitting out in the ultraviolet decaying in my absence. The mainsail is protected by its cover.

1915 I am now drinking a celebratory glass of wine in the cabin and the heavens have opened and it is pouring with rain! It is idyllic here on this little tributary to the Vilaine [despite the rain!]. Opposite to me are cows grazing in a field. Behind me the dense pine forest climbs steeply upwards.

2045 I have always been convinced that Almighty God knows what is best for me and he has bought me to Le Port de Foleux. I have now finished supper and had two glasses of Red wine!

2200 Turned in. There are still heavy showers of rain.

Tuesday the 13ᵗʰ of July, 2010.

0900 Got up and had a cup of tea. There has been a lot of heavy rain during the night.

0900---1130 Copied items from books, pilot etc. that I will need for my writing in the future.

1130---1200 Had a cup of coffee in the cockpit. It is extraordinary how apprehension can haunt you. I am now concerned about working the computer at the railway station so that I can get my ticket! This is absurd because what does it really matter? I'm safe!

The weather is very humid but warm.

1200---1600 Cleaned Ship.

1600 Went ashore for a shower.

1700 Went for a motor up my little river in the dinghy. There is another Heavenly Twins catamaran up there called the "Sally". She is a Mark IV version unlike the "Tarla" which is a Mark IIA.

1830 Went ashore, had a drink and then a very nice meal in the Bar/Cafe.

2030 Went and collected the marina boat which is like a shopping trolley. You put a euro into a gadget which releases a chain which means you can take the boat away. When you bring it back you get your euro back. Back on board the "Tarla" I deflated the dinghy and packed it away. I put the solar panels away. I set the alarm for 0500 as the taxi will be coming to the Capitanerie at 0600.

Checked and rechecked and worried that I have forgotten something vital.

2200 Turned in.

Wednesday 14ᵗʰ July, 2010. [Bastille Day].

0500 Got up. Rowed ashore and reclaimed my Euro.

0600 Taxi to Redon.

0830 TGV to Lille and Eurostar to London [Arrived London at 1515].

THE END

[POSTSCRIPT: I returned on September the 1st and joined a long queue outside the Capitanerie. There I managed to secure a contract for the use of a mooring from April to September 2011 for about 500 Euro. I also arranged with la Cale de Neptune to lift the "Tarla" out during the second week of September and to store her ashore until April 2011 (Cost about 1000 Euro). Chloé in the Capitanerie and Jean-François in La Cale de Neptune proved particularly helpful].

APPENDIX

I

PSYCHOLOGY

"Man lives in a world of objects, which influence him, and which he desires to influence; therefore he ought to know these objects in their nature, in their conditions, and in their relations with each other and mankind".

Froebel, cited in Michaelis and Moore, 1915, p.68.

"The two separate worlds of the seaman and the landsman must have developed very early in the course of mankind's encounter with the sea, and they persist as separate entities to the present day. The seaman's world is alien to the landsman unless he makes a lifetime study of it; the more so since the seaman's very alienation makes him difficult to communicate with, makes his world not only the "other", but also closed. Consequently, scholars whose lives have been involved with the history of the landsman have rightly been inclined to avoid the otherness of the world of seamen and boatmen." Basil Greenhill, The Archaeology of Boats and Ships (London, 1995, p.19).

Marin Marie, the great French single-handed sailor, in his book "Wind Aloft" has this to say:

"Almost any day, if you take the trouble, you may come across men alone in boats far out to sea off our coasts out of sight of land; old shellbacks (and there are young ones as well) who go out line fishing from morning to night, all alone without seeing anything sensational in it. They smoke their pipes, take a drink, talk all alone to themselves, in short they are sort of sea hermits".

"You come across him at sea, huddled over the tiller, apparently indifferent to all that might well happen, and when given a hail hardly bothering to lift a numbed arm; but his eyes are like needles, which rake the sea in every direction never letting him be caught out. If a squall comes he changes jibs and takes in a reef without worrying, mutters an oath for form's sake by all the thousand names of God, puts on oilskins and sea-boots---and that's all---"

[Manuscript delivered to the French publishers in 1939. Not published in English until 1945]

It would seem from my own experience that the above is still the case today. However, the thousands of small rowing and sailing boats of yesteryear have been replaced by thousands of small motor boats---but many of them still have the lone sailor who fishes. These people make up the majority of the remaining hunter-gatherers in the Western World.

I wrote the following analysis of my own psychological state on Sunday the 11th July, 2010 when I was tied up to the visitor's pontoon in the Port of Foleux the day before visiting "La Cale de Neptune" for the first time on Monday 12th of July to ask about Winter storage for the "Tarla".

"Fear, perhaps better described as apprehension. Lonely and frustrated but not while at sea because there is too much to do. When at sea slightly manic. I miss those that I love very much but I am fascinated by the sea. I fear it; but it can sometimes bring great rewards. Water has fascinated me since I was tiny. It has in one sense never been the life for me but the boats that sail on it have been a lifetime study. I can have too much of it but eventually I have this over-whelming desire to come back for another dose. I feel a great sense of achievement after a long voyage like this one but I am still worried that I won't pull it off ie: Find a safe place for the "Tarla" to stay for the Winter.

Waiting is the worst bit. Waiting for the weather or waiting to know whether they will accept the "Tarla" for the Winter. Then loneliness can start to affect you as you can be cooped up with only yourself as company. Many years ago I decided that the Merchant Navy was not a long term career for me because I could not bear the thought of having a wife and children and not being with them. I still feel the same about those that I love. I do not like being parted from them but there is always the "pull of the sea" working the other way".

Frank Mulville in his book "Single-handed Sailing" [Seafarer Books, London. 1990] says that:

"Sailing alone in some respects is a form of therapy for sufferers from the disease of modern living. It is not escapism---the lone sailor must place heavy reliance on the shore both for his physical and mental support. Neither is it a challenge or a defiance or a trip for the ego. At its most rewarding it is the simple, ordinary sailor's way of achieving perfection. It is certainly a test---of stamina, of mental resilience, of ingenuity and of adaptability. To be done properly it demands dedication on the part of the lone sailor, which we all have in common with all seekers after perfection".

Finally, the well known yachtsman Dixon Kemp wrote in 1891 concerning McMullan's last single-handed cruise in the 27 foot the "Persius" built in 1890.

"In the morning of the 13th (June, 1891), Mr. McMullan landed and posted a letter at Eastbourne. After this he boarded the "Perseus" again and went on down Channel. The next heard of him was a telegram on June 16, saying he was found dead on the evening of June 15 by some French fishermen. He was sitting in the cockpit, with his face looking towards the sky, and the vessel sailing herself along. The doctor said he had been dead for twenty-four hours when his body was found, the cause of death being failure of the heart's action. He must, therefore, have died in mid-Channel on Sunday night, the 14th of June. The weather was fine, the breeze light, and the young moon was shimmering on the placid sea. He was landed at Beuzeval (about six miles west of Trouville), and the Vice-Consul, Mr. A. O'Neill, at once communicated with his family and arranged for the funeral. Mrs. McMullan and his brother, Mr. J. McMullan, reached Beuzeval on the 18th, and Mr. R.T. McMullan was buried the next day in the cemetery at that place, after a simple service in the Protestant church."

In the Introduction to the 1893 Edition of R.T. McMullan's "Down Channel" Dixon Kemp says that:

"It can easily be believed that the end of Mr. McMullan was exactly as he would have wished it to be---when alone upon the sea". Mr. McMullan was sixty-one and I am sixty-four!

2

DESCRIPTION OF THE "TARLA"

[The following was written in 2003 by Mike McKimm,
a previous owner of the "Tarla" just before he sold her to
Michael Harrington from whom I purchased her in 2005].

General Description:
1976 Heavenly Twins Catamaran built by Constellation yachts.
GRP hull and deck. She is 26feet long X 13.75 feet wide X 2frt
6ins draft. Sloop rig with centre cockpit. Power by 4 stroke 9.9
Yahama ultra long shaft through cockpit sole. This is a strong
sea going cat, 3 of which have circumnavigated and literally
hundreds have gone down to the Med or Canaries. It has an
excellent safety record.

Accommodation is 6 berths in 3 cabins. The main saloon
provides a huge double berth when the dining table is folded
down. The two aft cabins each have a double berth. The saloon
has seating for 6-8 around a large table. Full standing headroom
is available in both hulls. The stb hull has a large navigation area
including half chart table with large drawer and endless storage
for equipment, books etc.

Condition:
The condition of the boat is good. There is some cosmetic
marking and chipping as decribed elsewhere and both keels
have seen grounding wear and tear but have been reasonably

maintained. The sails are good and much of the gear is just a couple of seasons old–including the engine which has seen less than 100 hours use since new.

Hulls/Deck etc.

The structure is all GRP except for a slatted foredeck which is in excellent condition. The topsides are a very light blue/green as was the favourite colour of the day–the hulls are white. The superstructure is remarkably free from any serious damage or chipping–given the age of the boat. I have reset most of the windows again to prevent leaks–a very successful operation. There is a tiny weep in severe conditions from the hatch on the saloon roof–so small it wasn't worth disturbing it and the interior lining. All fittings are sound and in good condition.

Both rudders are in very good condition and strongly mounted.

The hulls are also sound with no damage beyond the usual scratches and scores. The starboard hull has a horizontal stress crack in the gel coat where, I think, she leaned against another vessel–not an uncommon problem for cats in drying harbours.. There is also some scuffing near by but it is only cosmetic. I have left all of this–there is no filler or paint hiding any marks I found. The transom has been painted–but this is over the bridge-deck, it seems to have been cosmetic as a number of holes have been filled after steps, brackets etc were fitted and removed. I can find no sign of damage or repairs.

There is also a score under the bridge-deck on the port side which seems to have been made by a mooring buoy or sailing over a dinghy with an outboard or similar. Its not deep and has been crudely filled by a previous owner. I have just ignored it.

Both keels have suffered from drying out on rough ground. They hadn't been fitted with sacrificial shoes. I have now fitted two hefty mahogany shoes and repaired the keels properly. I do know that early in its life it was allowed to dry out in St.

Ives on rocks and the bottom edges of the keels were chewed up. But all have been soundly repaired and I have tidied them where necessary.

After I bought the boat, I took both hulls back to the gelcoat to examine them-so know them to be undamaged and free of osmosis.

The cockpit is self draining.

Rig & Rigging:

This is the standard sloop setup with an inner forestay and two separate backstays. The mast is stepped on the cabin roof by the edge of the cockpit, making it easy to work at. There is furler reefing on the genoa and the main is slab or roller reefed as you wish. All the reefing can be done from the cockpit making this a very safe boat to handle. Because of the wide aspect of the rig, it is very unstressed, compared to a narrower mono-hull.

Any work on the foredeck, such as rigging the storm sail or setting the cruising chute is very easy and safe due to the width of the deck.

There is a winch on the mast and winches on each side of the cockpit for the genoa. The main is controlled from a track fitted to the top of the rear cabin, and led back to the cockpit.

There are jackstays throughout the boat.

Sails:

The sails are generally in good condition. Any repairs have been done professionally and have been made, in my time, anyway, to attend to places of wear or damaged stitching. The sails set well, without much stretch. The storm sail is unused as is the cruising chute. The genoa has a UV protection strip.

Engine: (type & age and other notes)

I have fitted the recommended engine for the HT. Its a 10hp 4 stroke Yahama and has done two seasons although the engine is actually 4 years old. It wasn't used in its first year or this present year and has less than 100 hours use. This is visually apparent.

The engine is an ultra long shaft mounted in a transom in the cockpit. It almost touches the ground when the boat is dried and ensures that there is NO cavitation in bad seas. The previous engine, the same model but 12 years old, pushed the boat at about 1.5 knots against a F9 and I was very impressed.

The new engine is electric start with remote controls. Its got a 10A alternator and oil warning light on the control panel. The engine can be tilted to get all but the skeg out of the water for sailing and there is a GRP cover for the engine area.

I have rigged two separate 5 gallon fuel tanks, each with its own remote feed. These can be swapped over during a long run. It means no spilling petrol or smell and makes the boat very safe. Both tanks have their own fuel gauges and live in a vented cockpit locker.

One major advantage of this engine set up is the access it gives in an emergency. I picked up a wire on the prop just hours into the engine's life. Within minutes I had removed the engine and lifted it into the cockpit where I cleared the prop and within about 15 minutes the engine was back in and running. A new prop was subsequently fitted as the original one was chipped and is now a spare on the boat. Try that with an inboard!

Some people fit diesels in these boats but a vulnerable prop(s) and the sheer weight and accessibility would put me off. Fuel consumption for the Yahama is almost exactly 2 litres an hour at 5 knots for Tarla.

Galley/plumbing etc
The galley is huge---its about 8' long at least with full standing room. It comprises lots of storage and locker space, lots of working surfaces, a s/s sink and drainer. Water is from a Whale lever pump type tap. Water is in two flexible tanks in the bows-I think they are about 10 gallons. The stb one supplies the sink in the heads.

Cooking is on a brand new Techimpex cooker and grill. The oven has a glass door and temp gauge. I have also replaced all the gas pipe system, including the regulator. There is ample room in the galley for a fridge but none is fitted. The gas bottle is secured in a locker that drains overboard.

Toilet/washing:
The heads are large and spacious with a marine loo and sink and water tap (Whale type). There is room for a shower but none is fitted. Storage in this area is ample and I keep sails, spare sheets, etc in the lockers behind the heads.

Fenders/buckets etc.
Fenders, buckets, ropes, tools for the outboard, spare parts, etc are all included–including several extra petrol carriers, radar reflector, boat hook and so on. There is a folding s/s boarding ladder on the transom.

Misc. 1
Steering is wheel and cable to port rudder. The rudders are linked. The steering box was replaced last season.

It is worth noting that the storage in the HT is legendry. An inflatable can be stored below decks with vast personal baggage, sails and there is still endless amounts of room. The cockpit lockers contain petrol tanks, gas and ropes, buckets, etc and there is still enough room for outboards and boxes and so on. The foredeck lockers handle two anchors, chain and ropes and all the fenders.

Misc. 2
A lot of thought has been put into making the boat safe. I have developed bow and stern compartments which are filled with foam fragments. Secondary bulkheads below floor levels have been created and then each hull part filled to create considerable

buoyancy and prevent serious water ingress. This means that there are in effect 6 separate compartments. Only one can fill (assuming that there is only one hole in the hull) and they can't fill from hull to hull.

Each hull is drained to a sump that is pumped by its own large Whale gusher pump located in the stb locker in the cockpit. In this way almost any ingress of water can be controlled or even ignored. (This all comes from experience in a previous HT where a keel was badly holed (unknown to me) and the damage was only found at the end of the season-the foam in the keel had stopped the water getting in.

Extra information, history, notable sails etc etc.

I sail the boat single-handed and have had this and other HTs all around the Irish sea and further. Her last voyage was a long trip to the Hebrides and back in what could only be called rather nasty weather, including the Infamous Mull of Kintyre. In the event, I continued on to my first goal (Gigha) when other 32' mono-hulls abandoned the journey and ran off to Campbeltown. One night passage was made in fog using the engine and radar for 13 hours. It was my first serious use of radar (its just two seasons old) and it was excellent.

The boat's downside is a tight turn in a windy packed harbour-she can be a bit of a handful because she needs speed to turn as do most cats. But she is light enough to be walked about.

Her great advantage, especially when single-handed is ease of handling and sailing upright, so you don't get tired. As a family boat, she is excellent-there is so much room and she is very safe.

The power is all 12V.

Strip lights are in all the cabins, the galley and the navigation area. Power is also fed to the control box in the cockpit where the VHF radio, radar, sounder and log are all powered and switched from. There is also a twin power socket by the navigation table to charge mobile phones, torches etc.

Navigation is covered by a Ritchie compass, Nasa log and sounder, JRC 1000 radar (which is ideal for this size of boat) VHF radio. There is also an Auto-helm 3000 wheel pilot. I have kept the controls together and boxed all the electrics in a protective shelter in the cockpit. In bad weather or when single-handing, its ideal beside the wheel.

All electrics to this area and the mast are hardwired to avoid joins, corroded plugs, etc. To allow the mast to be removed the one connection is made within a plastic protective box mounted out of harms way. It proved very successful and I would never have plugs again.

On the mast there is a tri-light and anchor light, steaming light, deck spot, radar with proper strut and safety cable. The cable for the the radar runs outside the mast to avoid the large holes that have to be cut to feed the cable plugs. I have also fitted Barton folding mast steps to give access to the trees and the radar.

There are also deck level navigation lights but I don't use them, so they are not all wired into the system (but can be).

Ground tackle/warps:
Chain and Anchorplait systems are on board for a CQR and Danforth anchor. A fisherman's anchor and further cable are stored below decks as a backup. There is ample rope on board (the boat is in effect ready for the sea but wasn't launched at the last minute). Again, because of the wide foredeck, anchoring and recovery is very easy.

Electrical/Navigation.
Almost all the boat has been completely rewired (except for some internal lights). Two batteries are fitted but there is room for more if required. However, I found that the engine more than recharged the batteries and even on long journeys I was never short of power, even if using the radar. The batteries are switched through the usual rotary switch.

3

WORK DONE ON THE TARLA SINCE THE ABOVE WAS WRITTEN.

Since coming into my ownership in 2005 the Tarla's hull has been completely overhauled, scratches in the hull made good, new bronze sea-cocks fitted and the hull and deck repainted. The area above the cabin door has been reinforced to take the compression load of the mast. Her keels have been fitted with stainless steel shoes. Her windows and hatch have been replaced with new ones. Her mast, rig and sails have been renewed (She is now cutter rigged). Her mainsail is 140 square feet, her staysail 40 square feet and her Jib 170 square feet. Both headsails are on roller furlers and her mainsail lowers into a bag suspended from lazy-jacks. Her flat cut spinnaker is 270 square feet and is shaped like an equilateral triangle. She has been fitted with a Solé Diesel with hydraulic drive to each hull (see below). The marine toilet has been removed and replaced with a portable toilet. The flexible water-tanks have been replaced with four 20 litre plastic cans which can be filled from the deck and pump to a tap. The advantage is that they can be taken out and cleaned at the end of the season. The boat has been completely rewired and she now has two 120 AH batteries for domestic use and a 70AH battery to start the engine. Two 32 watt solar panels have been installed to power the former and a 15 watt panel to top up the latter. The engine alternator also charges the batteries. She is also wired for mains electricity. Almost all the electrical equipment with the exception of the radar has been replaced with new units. She has all new navigational equipment (except the Furuno GPS and NASA Navtex). The inside of the cabin has been lined with 9mm cork tiles and the main and forward bulkheads have been panelled with teak ply and iroko strips. She has "Eberspracher" central heating. She carries four new anchors (2 X 16kg; 1 X 10kg; 1 X 5kg)) with their respective chain and rope. The Techinpex stove has been connected with new piping to camping gas bottles in a special box in the forward port chain locker. The previous owner Michael Harrington installed a new fridge in the galley.

4

EQUIPMENT CARRIED ON THE VOYAGE

An indication of the equipment carried can be seen from the following "RNLI SEACHECK LIST".

Priority Equipment
Anchors with warp/chain & strong point. YES.
Radar Reflector YES.
Appropriate Navigation Lights YES.
Appropriate Day Shapes YES.
Appropriate Sound Signals YES.
Lifebuoy or similar YES.
MOB Recovery Equipment YES.
Inflatable Dinghy YES.
Life Raft NO. XXX
Emergency Steering YES.
Kill Cord for dinghy outboard motor NO. XXX
Alternative means of propulsion/starting YES.
Appropriate tool kit and spares YES.
Lifejackets 150N min per person YES.
Safety Harnesses and means of attachment YES.
Bailer/Bucket YES.
Bucket & Hand Bilge Pump YES.
Charts, Almanac, Pilots and Plotting Instruments YES.
Table of Emergency Signals YES.
Compass YES.
VHF (fixed) YES.
VHF (handheld) YES.

EPIRB YES.
Torch/Spotlight YES.
Appropriate Flares YES.
Fire Blanket YES.
Fire Extinguishers YES.
Smoke Alarm YES.
Temporary Hull Repair Kit YES.
First Aid Kit YES.

Recommended Equipment
Fairlead for anchor warp YES.
Towing Warp and Fenders YES.
Kedge Anchor YES.
Sea Anchor/ Heavy Warps YES.
Throwing Line/ Rescue Quoit   NO. XXX
Boarding Ladder YES.
Dan Buoy NO. XXX
LW/MW Radio Receiver YES.
Additional handheld VHF YES.
Navtex YES.
HF/Satcom NO. XXX
Emergency Aerial NO. XXX
Barometer YES.
Echo Sounder YES.
GPS or equivalent YES.
Hand bearing compass YES.
Log YES.
Binoculars YES.
Personal protective warm clothing YES.
Emergency Grab Bag and Emergency Water YES.
Emergency Knife YES.
Storm Sails YES.
Emergency repair materials YES.
Means of severing rigging NO. XXX

5

THE ENGINE

The engine is a Solé Diesel (3 cylinder) 27HP installed in the cockpit driving two hydraulic motors fitted with Brunton two bladed autoprops. According to the graph produced by the manufacturers 27.2 HP is produced at the maximum speed of 3600 revs and uses a maximum of 4.5 litres per hour at this speed. Maximum torque occurs at 2200 revs and fuel consumption is 1 litre per hour (I presume with the engine not under load). The engine is currently set for a maximum of 2200 revs when under load although this reduces the available horsepower to 20.

There has been an ongoing saga with the engine since it was installed four years ago. There turned out to be two problems:

The size of the return hoses from the hydraulic motors in each hull were the same size as the inlet hoses. They were eventually replaced with larger hoses to reduce the back pressure.

There was a faulty control valve switching the hydraulic fluid to the motors so that most of the latter was not going to the motors but was bypassing with the diesel engine just revving away with no load on it when the full drive should have been transmitted to the propellers.

It is now possible by turning a screw with an Allen key (having first loosened the locknut) to adjust the top speed of the engine for maximum drive and economy.

In the river near Tréguier I carried out speed trials in almost flat calm conditions and achieved the following results:

> 1000 revs---3.7 knots
> 1200 revs---4.4 knots
> 1400 revs---5.0 knots
> 1600 revs---5.7 knots
> 1800 revs---6.2 knots
> 2200 revs---7.0 knots

Thus top speed under either power or sail is about 7 knots. I did however touch 7.5 knots beating down the River Deben a couple of years ago!

Speed is measured by a "Tack Tick" speedometer which has been calibrated from a Stowe trailing log/speedometer which I have found in the past to be extremely accurate.

With the weight of the diesel engine, hydraulic system, fuel and water, anchors and chain, tools, sails, dinghies, spare parts etc. The "Tarla" is at least two inches lower in the water than when I bought her. The Diesel/hydraulic system is obviously much heavier than the Honda 10 HP outboard that she had when I purchased her. The main gain has been the much increased manoeuvrability in the marina.

6

PERFORMANCE

I t would be very interesting to work out the frictional and residual resistance for one of the HT hulls and double the result. Further calculations could be made with respect to the prismatic coefficient (Ratio of the immersed volume to the area of the mid-ship section X waterline length), J.E. Paris' relationship between prismatic coefficient and lateral plane coefficient and some type of adapted Rayner analysis for when the catamaran was heeled. It would seem to me, purely from close inspection of the hulls that the prismatic co-efficient must be about 0.6 and the half angle of entrance at the waterline about 10 degrees.

With respect to the shape of each hull one would need the offsets from the original drawing. In their absence one can only measure the principal dimensions. These were given in a boat-test of the Heavenly Twins Catamaran by "Boat" magazine April 1977 [The "Tarla" was built in 1976] and are as follows: Length overall---26ft 2 ins. Length waterline 21ft 6ins. Beam 13ft 9ins. Draft 2ft 3ins. Sail Areas: Mainsail 140 square feet. Working jib 120 square feet. Genoa 200 square feet. The basic hull and deck mouldings are reported as weighing 3,500 lbs. Under the heading "Construction" the article has this to say:

"The strength of the vessel is derived in part from the weight of her reinforced mouldings, but also from the fact that these number only two, and that they incorporate centre cockpit layout. In addition to the forward bulkhead, we therefore have two substantial bulkheads amidships, which in a cat is exactly where we need them. The large 'U' section thus created sits firmly athwart the hulls and gives tremendous rigidity.

In the deck this is a 9 oz moulding which includes a 2 oz woven roving, while in the hulls a nominally 8 oz lay is raised to 12 oz at the keels, and at the junction between hull and bridge deck; a 2 oz woven roving is included throughout. Such figures as these may be often quoted, but this yacht seems one of the few where one can jump on a coach-roof with a span of 10 feet and hear a most reassuring 'thump'."

"With a rising sun the wind served, though not more than about Force 2, but with the Genoa set we could settle down to some horizontal sailing, here at about 4 knots. In these fair conditions the boat points surprisingly well---on the compass, within 50 degrees. As I mentioned earlier, going about is to some extent pre-determined by the angular range of the rudders, so one may put the helm down quite hard but scarcely disturb her leisurely transition to the other tack."

The Tarla's displacement is given as 6250 lbs in the sales "blurb" and I presume this figure refers to the maximum all up weight when loaded with stores, fuel, gear and human beings. It is to be noted that by subtracting the weight of the mouldings from this figure one is left with 2750 lbs for all equipment, gear and people. I am sure that the Sóle diesel, currently fitted, with its fuel and hydraulic motors will weigh in at 600 lbs. The mast, rigging and sails probably 500 lbs. Anchors chain and warp 300 lbs and so on!

As measured by me with the "Tarla" ashore the following information can be used to give an idea of her shape.

Underneath the hull the Bridge-deck is 6ft wide at its narrowest point. The nacelle is 3ft wide which leaves 18ins either side which are reinforced with 'U' shaped mouldings 4 ½ ins wide and 2 ½ ins deep set in the middle of the 18ins panel and running longitudinally. For most of its length the nacelle is 3ft wide and is of squashed 'U' shape being 12ins deep. The nacelle starts 3ft 6ins back from the bow when viewed in profile. [This is 1ft aft of the bow waterline]. It reaches its full depth and width 6ft back from the bow.

The hulls appear to have a maximum beam of about 4ft and are at their broadest point 10ft aft of the bow waterline and 12ft forward of the stern waterline. From the side profile the position of greatest depth [lowest point of "rocker"] of the 'U' shaped hulls is approx. 7ft 8ins aft of the bow waterline. Moving the buoyancy well forward and having hulls which are "cod's head and mackerel tailed" does much to stop pitch polling. However, the very fine sterns do little to stop "hobby-horsing" which is a well known characteristic of Heavenly Twins Catamarans in certain conditions.

The keels have a bottom which is parallel to the waterline and commence with a slight slope aft 7ft 8ins behind the bow waterline [or 10 foot 2ins aft of the bow]. They are streamlined with a thickness of 2ins at their forward end, 5ins in the middle and 3ins at their after end. They commence 7ft 8ins aft of the bow waterline [at the same point as the maximum "rocker" of the 'U' shaped hulls]. They are 11feet long which includes the slope aft at 45 degrees [the length of this slope being 2ft 6ins]. At their forward end they protrude 9 ½ ins below the 'U' shaped hull [this will almost be the point of rotation which is 1/3 of the waterline length aft of the bow]. Aft of the keels it is 3ft 2ins to the aft waterline and this includes the skegs but does not include the rudders which are 18ins long at the waterline. This gives a waterline length on the "Tarla" of 21ft 10ins and 23ft 4ins if you include the rudders. The draft measures 2ft 8 ½ins and this includes the stainless steel shoes which have been fitted to the bottom of the keels. At this draft the nacelle is just "kissing" the water. At the aft waterline the stern-post slopes back a further 22ins to give an overall hull length of 26ft 2ins.

The appendix to Michael McMullan's book "Multihull Seamanship" [Nautical Publishing 1976] shows the speed/length ratios for multi-hulls and mono-hulls in the 1974 Round Britain Race. The speed/length ratio is calculated by dividing the speed in knots by the square root of the waterline length in feet. This is one measure of a vessel's efficiency. What is fascinating is that a Heavenly Twins catamaran took part and completed this 1885 mile race coming 37th out of the 40 to finish. Her average speed for the entire trip was 3.4 knots and her speed length ratio based on this result was 0.731.

The "most efficient sailing vessel" was the trimaran the "Three Legs of Man" which had an overall length of 35ft, a waterline length of 33.75ft. She averaged 6.82 knots, more than twice that of the HT, and had a speed length ratio of 1.172.

When one looks at the fastest leg of the race for a particular vessel [there are five legs] one finds that the HT averaged 4.33 knots for the 420 miles from Castlebay to Lerwick (giving a speed length ratio of 0.931) while the "Three Legs of Man" averaged 7.88 knots for the 460 miles from Crosshaven to Castlebay (a speed length ratio of 1.354).

The slowest leg for the HT was from Crosshaven to Castlebay when she averaged 2.88 knots giving a speed length ratio of 0.619. While the slowest leg for the "Three Legs of Man" was from Plymouth to Crosshaven (230 miles) in leg one when she averaged 5.53 knots giving a speed length ratio of 0.950. So the "efficiency of the HT on her fastest leg was almost identical to that of "Three Legs of Man" on her slowest. Much of this difference was caused by the difference in their weight/length ratio and their relative waterline beam to waterline length ratio. The "Three Legs of Man" weighed no more than the HT although she was more than 12 feet longer on the waterline. Waterline length defines maximum speed. The accepted wisdom being that a displacement hull cannot easily exceed the square root of their waterline length in feet multiplied by 1.34. This means that the "Tarla" has a maximum speed of 6.2 knots. When she achieves 7 knots the multiplier rises to 1.5. The Tarla's waterline beam for each hull is about 4 foot which is about the same as the "Three Legs of Man's" main hull. The length beam ratio of the former is approx. 5.4 while the latter is approx 8.4. As the trimaran heels she will tend to lift her main hull out of the water making the length/beam ratio more like 10:1. It is well known that long thin hulls with a 10:1 ratio can exceed the restriction imposed by the general rule of the square root of the waterline length multiplied by 1.34. The HT's speed is thus limited by her beam and weight but on the other hand they contribute greatly to her seaworthiness.

The least efficient vessel to complete the 1974 Round Britain Race was a mono-hull called the "Eclipse of Mylor" with an overall length of 28 feet and a waterline length of 24 feet. She averaged 2.62 knots over the 1885 miles to give a speed length ratio of 0.535. Lest it be thought that mono-hulls cannot be "efficient" the "Chough of Parkstone"[30feet length overall, 21feet length waterline] averaged 4.58 knots over the total distance giving a speed length ratio of 1.076.

Finally, a comparison with the "Minnetaree" [a Mark Two Iroquois Catamaran built by Sailcraft of Brightlingsea] proves interesting. She completed the 1885 miles at an average speed of 4.37 knots giving a speed length ratio of 0.840. Her overall length was 30ft and her waterline length 27 feet. She weighed less than the Heavenly Twins.

If one takes the speed/length ratio of the "Three Legs of Man" as 100% then the others mentioned above can be rated as follows:

The "Ecipse of Mylor"(M) 53%
The"Heavenly Twins"(C) 69%
The"Minnetaree"(C) 83%

The"Chough of Parkstone"(M) 92%
The"Three Legs of Man"(T) 100%

As mentioned above this gives one measure of their efficiency as sailing vessels.

7

STATISTICS – COSTS OF MARINA BERTHS etc. [June/July 2010]

(The "Tarla" is 8 metres long & 4.2 metres wide).

Unless otherwise stated the charges below were for berthing alongside a pontoon with direct access to the shore.

RAMSGATE---£19-20 per night. Total £38-40. No surcharge for catamarans.

EASTBOURNE [Sovereign Harbour]---£23-00 per night. Total £230-00. No surcharge for catamarans. Purchased 56 litres of diesel for £50-07. Purchased 5 litres of petrol for £6-46 & a camping gas cylinder refill for £21-95.

BEMBRIDGE [I.O.W.]---£20-00 per night. Total £40. No surcharge for catamarans.

CHERBOURG---Euro 18-00 per night. Total Euro 36. No surcharge for catamarans. 20% discount if you belong to a recognised yacht club which I didn't. Euro2 per "Jeton" for each shower. Purchased 20 litres of diesel for Euro 24-20.

GUERNSEY---£18-00 per night for a berth on a pontoon in the middle of the harbour with no direct access to the shore. No surcharge for catamarans.

TRÉGUIER---Euro 21-20 per night. Total Euro 42-40. No surcharge for catamarans. Free showers. Free electricity. Purchased 10 litres of diesel for Euro 11-20.

TRÉBEURDEN---Euro 23-00 per night. Total Euro 23-00. No surcharge for catamarans. Euro 1 for a "Jeton" for a shower.

L'ABERWRAC'H---Euro 20-60 per night. Total Euro 82-40. No surcharge for catamarans. Free showers. Purchased 40 litres of diesel for Euro 48-00. Facilities excellent.

CAMERET---Euro 26-25 per night. Total Euro 52-50. Charge calculated on a formula involving length x breadth. Facilities not great.

ÎLE DE GOIX [Port Tudy]---Euro 13-00 for mooring to buoys in the centre of the harbour. No surcharge for catamarans. Total Euro 13-00.

ÉTEL---Euro 22-00 per night. Total Euro 44-00. Charge calculated on a formula involving length x breadth.

FOLEUX---Euro 14 per night. Total Euro 28. Charge calculated on a formula involving length x breadth. Contract to lay to a buoy from the 12th of July until the 31st August cost Euro 118-00.

TOTALS

TOTAL COST OF BERTHING FOR 31 NIGHTS:--- £326-40 + Euro 321-30. This is an approximate average of 22 Euro per night. The remaining 5 nights were spent at anchor free of charge. Therefore 16% of nights were spent at anchor at a saving of approx. 100 Euro.

CONSUMPTION OF DIESEL---126 LITRES [The tank was roughly at the same level at the end of the trip as when I started].

TOTAL COST OF DIESEL: £50-07 + Euro 83-40.

8

STATISTICS – DISTANCE, TIME, AVERAGE SPEED, ENGINE REVS etc.

[Note these statistics include tidal influences and other variables that affect the performance of a vessel such as wave height and swell]

WALTON TO RAMSGATE (Pegwell Bay). Distance 55 miles. Time 10.5 hrs. Average speed 5.2 knots. Motor-sailing the whole way. Engine Revs: 3hrs @ 1400 revs. 7.5 hrs @ 1200 revs. Average revs 1257.

RAMSGATE TO EASTBOURNE (Sovereign Harbour). Distance 66 miles. Time 14hrs. Average speed 4.7 knots. Motor-sailing the whole way. Engine revs: 5hrs @ 1500 revs. 5hrs @ 1400 revs. 2hrs @ 1000 revs. 2hrs @ 1300 revs. Average revs 1364.

EASTBOURNE TO BEMBRIDGE I.O.W. Distance 63 miles. Time 14hrs. Average speed 4.5 knots. 8hrs under sail only. Distance 37.5 miles. 6hrs motor-sailing. Distance 25.5 miles. Under sail only: 2hrs @5.5kns (F4). 3hrs @ 5kns (F3). 1hr @ 4.5kns (F2/3). 2hrs @ 3.5kns (F2). Average speed under sail: 4.7 knots. Engine revs: 1hr @ 1300 revs. 1hr @ 1000 revs. 1hr @ 1100 revs. 2hrs @ 1200 revs. 1hr @ 1600 revs. Average Revs: 1233. Average speed motor-sailing 4.25 knots.

BEMBRIDGE TO CHERBOURG. Distance 66 miles direct (83 miles through the water). Time 17.5 hours. Average speed 3.8 knots (4.7 knots through the water). 5.5 hours under sail only. Distance 37.5 miles. 12 hours motor-sailing. Distance 45.5

miles. Under sail only: 2hrs @ 5.5 knots (F4). 1hr @ 4.5kns (F2/3). 2.5hrs @ 3.5kns (F2). Average speed under sail: 4.4 knots. Engine revs: 12hrs @ 1400 revs. Average revs 1400. Average speed motor-sailing 3.8 knots.

CHERBOURG TO GUERNSEY. Distance 43 miles (33 miles through the water). Time 6.5 hours. Average speed 6.6 knots (5.1 knots through the water). Motor-sailing the whole way. Engine revs: 6.5hrs @ 1400 revs. Average revs 1400. There was little wind for the voyage. Almost a flat calm with smooth sea.

GUERNSEY TO TRÉGUIER. Distance 52 miles. Time 12hrs. Average speed 4.3 knots. Under sail only: 1hr @ 3kns. 11hrs motor-sailing with an average speed of 4.5kns. Engine revs: 11hrs @1400 revs. Average revs 1400.

TRÉGUIER TO TRÉBEURDEN. Distance 35 miles (25 miles through the water). Time 7.5 hours. Average speed 4.7kns. (3.3kns through the water). 1.5hrs under sail only with an average speed of 2kns. 6hrs motor sailing at an average speed of 3.7 knots. Engine revs: 1hr @1000 revs. 3hrs @ 1400 revs. 2hrs @ 1000 REVS. Average revs 1200. The reason for the low speed through the water was due to "hobby-horsing".

TRÉBEURDEN TO L'ABERWRAC'H. Distance 49 miles. Time 11 hours. Average speed 4.5 knots. 1hr under sail only with an average speed of 3kns. During 10 hrs of motor-sailing made good 46 miles at an average speed of 4.6 knots. Engine revs: 2.5hrs @ 1400revs. 1hr @ 1250revs. 1hr @ 1400revs. 1hr @ 1200revs. 1hr @ 1400revs. 2hrs @1500revs. 1hr @ 1600revs. 0.5hrs @ 1000revs. Average revs 1235.

L'ABERWRAC'H TO CAMERET. Distance 34 miles. Time 7.5 hours. Average speed 4.5 knots. Engine revs: 2hrs @ 1400revs. 2hrs @ 1300revs. 3.5hrs at 1400revs. Average revs 1373. Higher than usual revs required due to very lumpy sea at the start. There was almost a flat calm.

CAMERET TO ÎLE DE GLÉNAN. Distance 55 miles. Time 13 hours. Average speed 4.2 knots. During 3 hours under sail made good 11 miles by log (F 2/3). Average speed 3.7 knots. During 10 hours motor-sailing made good 44 miles. Average speed 4.4 knots. Engine Revs: 3hrs @ 1200revs. 2hrs @ 1000revs. 2hrs @1400revs. 3hrs @1200revs. Average revs 1200. Slowed down to wait for the tidal window at the Raz du Sein.

ÎLE DE GLÉNAN TO ÎLE DE GOIX. Distance 22 miles. Time 5hrs. Average speed 4.4 knots. Engine revs: 1hr @ 1000revs. 4hrs @ 1200revs. Average revs 1160. Almost a flat calm.

ÎLE DE GOIX TO ÉTEL. Distance 10 miles. Time 4 hours. Average speed 2.5 knots. Engine Revs: 2hrs @1000revs. 1hr @1000revs. Average revs 1000. 1 hour was spent drifting with all sail up waiting for the tide to rise over Étel bar. No distance covered as it was a flat calm. Average speed under power 3.3 knots.

ÉTEL TO HOUAT. Distance 23 miles. Time 5hrs. Average speed 4.6 knots. Under sail only "Tarla" covered 21.40 miles as measured by the Stowe trailing log in 4 hours giving an average speed under sail of 5.4 knots. Highest speed measured under sail 6.9 knots while beating into a Force 4 wind off Étel. Engine Revs: 0.66hrs @ 1800revs. 0.33hrs @ 1800 revs. Average revs 1800. Highest speed recorded under power 6kns while crossing the Étel bar against a strong incoming tide and a Force 4 headwind.

HOUAT TO ARZAL. Distance 23.5 miles. Time 6 hours. Average speed 3.9 knots. Under sail only 1.5hrs @ average speed of 2.7 knots. Under power 4.5hrs @ 4.3 knots. Engine revs 4.5hrs @ 1000revs. Average revs 1000.

ARZAL TO FOLEUX. Distance 8.75 miles. Time 2.75 hours. Average speed 3.2 knots. Running under jib only in the smooth water of the river with a following wind of Force 2/3.

TOTALS

Total distance voyaged under power and sail from Walton to Foleux 622.5 miles. Total time underway 136.25 hours. Average speed 4.6 knots.

Under Sail

Total distance 129 miles. Total time spent sailing 29.25 hours. Average speed under sail 4.4 knots. Percentage of total time under sail 22%. Percentage of total distance covered under sail 21%.

Under Power and Sail.

Total Distance 493 miles. Total time spent motor-sailing 107 hours. Average speed 4.6 knots.

Percentage of total time under power and sail 78%.

Percentage of total distance covered under power and sail 79%.

Engine

Total number of revs 133890. Total time under power 107 hours. Average revs 1251.3.

Fuel Consumption.

107 hours of motor sailing used 126 litres of diesel (At a total cost of approx. 150 Euro). Therefore fuel consumption was 1.17 litres per hour. (At 1250 revs the manufacturers fuel consumption is given as 0.2 litres per hour!). The cost per hour is approximately 1 Euro 40.

493 miles were covered using 126 litres of fuel. This gives 3.9 nautical miles per litre. The cost per mile being approximately 30 cents.

9
COMMENT ON APPENDIX
EIGHT ABOVE

The striking points about the above are:

The lack of wind and the time spent motor-sailing.

The average speed under sail only is almost the same as the average (economical) speed under power.

The average speed for passage planning is 4.5 knots.

The fuel consumption under power is very low.

10

"PLUS POINTS" AND "MINUS POINTS" FOR THE VOYAGE.

"PLUS POINTS"

Fridge

Solar Panels

Engine

Roller Reefing Headsails

Chart-Plotter

"Tack-Tick " combined speed depth wireless system.

"Delta" 15kg Anchor.

"MINUS POINTS"

Fully battened mainsail can only be lowered when head to the wind---otherwise sticks.

Autopilot cannot cope unless conditions are ideal.

11

LIST OF PICTURES IN THIS BOOK

The following ten pictures of the voyage are included after Chapter Three in the order:

Picture of the "Tarla" in Eastbourne (Sovereign Harbour)

The "Arklow Wind" which I passed at sea off the Isle of White.

"Le Vieux Copain" in Cherbourg Harbour.

The Château at Tréguier under which Tom Cunliffe rode out Hurricane Charlie in 1986.

Peter Spry-Leverton arrives in L'Aberwrac'h aboard the "Anadina".

Dolphins in the Baie de Audienne.

The Îles de Glénan.

Port Tudy, Île de Goix.

The Île de Huout

Le Port de Foleux.

In addition, after Appendix Twelve, there is a plan of an HT taken from "Boat" Magazine (April 1977, page 51) and there are four pictures of the "Tarla"--- one afloat in Bedwell's Boatyard, Walton-on-the-Naze Essex. and three ashore. These give a clear idea of the shape of the hull.

12

CHART OF THE VOYAGE

Chart of "Tarla"'s voyage 2010

A / B Anchor / warps
C   Forepeak stowage
D / E Dinette, double berth
F   Lockers

G   Motor
H   Double berths
K   Chart Table
L   Galley

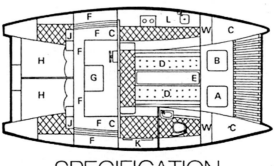

SPECIFICATION

L.O.A.	26ft 2in
L.W.L.	21ft 6in
Beam	13ft 9in
Draft	2ft 3in
Sail Areas	
Main	140 sq ft
Working Jib	120 sq ft
Genoa	200 sq ft

Standard spec. includes: Pulpit and lifelines, storm jib, 25lb CQR, 3 fathoms of chain and 150 ft nylon warp, fluorescent cabin lighting, chart lamp, fuse box, deck socket, navigation lights, gas bottle, compass, two 60 ft and two 40 ft polypropylene warps, sea toilet.

Extras include: Genoa, bilge pump, sail cover, H.D. battery, refrigerator, boom tent, twin forestays.

Standard engine: Yamaha 28 hp outboard with Morse single lever control and electric start, all fitted to the boat   £820
Standard boat, ex engine   £7,750
De Luxe boat, ex engine   £8,350
Hull and deck bonded with bulkheads, locker bottoms, athwartship timbers and toilet door   £3,620

All prices ex VAT.
Aquarius Marine, The Quay, Gweek, Helston, Cornwall. Tel: Mawgan 696.

This is a plan of a HT taken from "Boat" Magazine (April 1977, page 51). The "Tarla" was built in 1976 and has an identical plan.

"Tarla" in Bedwell's Boatyard, Walton-On-Naze, Essex.
Before being repainted.

"Tarla" ashore in Eastbourne before I purchased her. The shape of the
Heavenly Twins' hull can be clearly seen here.

"Tarla" ashore in Bedwell's Boatyard, Walton-On-Naze, Essex.
Showing shape of underwater lines.

"Tarla" ashore in Bedwells. Note the brunton auto-prop and the
stainless steel keel shoe and extension